But Nobody Told Me
I'd Ever Have to Leave Home

But Nobody Told Me
I'd Ever Have to Leave Home

From Toddlers to Teens: How Parents Can Raise Children
to Become Capable Adults

KATHY LYNN

foreword by Linda Lewis
editor-in-chief
Today's Parent magazine

whitecap

Edited by Holly Bennett
Copyedited by Ben D'Andrea
Proofread by Nicola Aimé
Cover design by Roberta Batchelor
Interior design by Margaret Lee /bamboosilk.com

Printed and bound in Canada by Friesens.

Library and Archives Canada Cataloguing in Publication

Lynn, Kathy, 1946–
  But nobody told me I'd ever have to leave home: from toddlers to teens : how parents
can raise children to become capable adults / Kathy Lynn.

ISBN 1-55285-703-4

  1. Parenting. 2. Autonomy in children. 3. Child rearing. I. Title.
HQ769.L95 2005   649'.7   C2005-903044-5

The publisher acknowledges the support of the Canada Council and the Cultural
Services Branch of the Government of British Columbia in making this publication
possible. We acknowledge the financial support of the Government of Canada through
the Book Publishing Industry Development Program for our publishing activities.

To my husband John, who is my biggest supporter, closest friend and the best Dad in the world.

To my favorite daughter, Chelsea, and my favorite son, Foley. My children taught me to avoid labels. Each is uniquely their own person. Chelsea is strong, independent and athletic, and Foley is a little bit geek and a little bit jock.

My family is my rock. Without them I wouldn't be the person I am. Daily, I thank them for being in my life.

CONTENTS

ACKNOWLEDGEMENTS

An author writes a book, but its production relies on the support, guidance and help of many. Without them, this book wouldn't exist.

I wish to thank my family for permission to tell their stories. A special thanks goes to my children, Chelsea and Foley, who took time from their busy lives to write the Afterword.

Terri Cody, a program advisor and instructor in the Early Childhood Education program at Lethbridge Community College, lent her expertise on play to Chapter One. She really knows her stuff, and she happens to be my sister.

Chelsea, Foley, my husband John, and friends Maureen Donlevy and Peter Jackson helped choose the title.

A very special thanks goes to Holly Bennett, my editor. She's my friend, my conscience, my guide, my cheerleader, and still finds time to do a superlative editing job. This book is as much hers as it is mine.

To Linda Lewis, editor-in-chief at *Today's Parent* magazine for writing the Foreword. Canadian parents have a great resource in *Today's Parent* magazine.

Everyone at Whitecap Books is a pleasure to work with. Each of them is responsive, respectful and helpful. Thank you for publishing my books.

FOREWORD

It was one of those mundane issues in family life that can frustrate even the most patient parent. A few years ago, when bedtime became a sore point between me and my son, I felt baffled until I happened to reread some advice in the pages of the parenting magazine I edit and had an "Aha!" moment. Not surprisingly, the source of my inspiration was one of *Today's Parent*'s most popular columnists, parent educator Kathy Lynn.

Her message was simple and sane. She asked, When was the last time you adjusted your child's bedtime? Is his bedtime arbitrary? Maybe he just needs a later one as he gets older and his needs change. In my family's case, she was so right.

In *But Nobody Told Me I'd Ever Have to Leave Home*, as in her monthly Ask Us magazine column, Kathy provides parents with many "Aha!" moments. With common sense and experience as her guide, she guides us on the path toward our children's maturity (and our own, too), gently reminding us that our kids' job is to test the limits and ours is to let them, in a safe and sane way. Through real-life scenarios, straightforward Q&As and easily digested advice, Kathy teaches us how to raise kids who are ready to find their own way in the world. That's our job. As she puts it, "The trip from total dependence to independence starts with the first breath your newborn takes."

Her perspective is often reassuring. Peer pressure isn't always a bad thing" is one of her comforting observations for families with teens. And it's refreshing, laced with Kathy's typical candor: "We run the risk of making children's play so organized, supervised and academic that the value of play gets lost." Most importantly, Kathy's wise words are useful. Having worked with Kathy Lynn for twelve years, I know this as an editor. But I especially know this as a mom.

Linda Lewis

Linda Lewis joined the *Today's Parent* editorial
staff as managing editor in 1993, and has been
editor-in-chief of the magazine since 1998.

INTRODUCTION

The plan for this book came about as I was writing *Who's in Charge Anyway? How Parents Can Teach Children to Do the Right Thing*.

I often see posters that say that when we raise children we need to give them roots and wings. My first book talked about giving them roots. In that book I told parents that they need to set the standards of their children's behavior and that when our kids have the security of knowing there's a caring and thoughtful adult in charge, they'll be able to get on with the job of developing into healthy adulthood.

This second book is about the wings. When a child is born, the first sign of health and life is the sound of her cry as she takes her first breath. Until this time she has been a part of her mother; they have been one and now they are two. This breath is the start of your child's independence.

As we give our children roots, we need to understand that these roots are designed to give kids the strength to eventually fly on their own. This book will tell you how to help them become capable adults and fly to independence.

For me, the final flight took place at the airport. First we put our oldest, Chelsea, on a plane to Montreal. She'd just finished high school and was traveling across the country for university. It was both difficult and simple to let her go. I didn't want to see her leave. I'd miss her, and I'd worry about her. On the other hand, she was ready; it was time for her to move to the next level of her development. The worst day for me was Thanksgiving. I love to celebrate with friends and family sitting around the dining room table, enjoying a great meal and conversation. But one chair was empty. I survived and knew that the days of having my kids with me all the time were really over, and it meant I had done my job.

Two years later, at the airport once again, we became true empty nesters. After a summer at home in Vancouver, Chelsea headed back to Montreal for her third year and her brother boarded a plane for Ottawa. Oh dear, now we had let the baby go. Was he ready?

Well, almost—but he did have some lessons to learn. He found accommodation in a house with three other students. Shortly thereafter we got a phone call. His voice, filled with outrage, bellowed loud and clear down the phone lines, "Do you guys have any idea what cheese costs?" Okay, there are some things they can only learn from experience.

I'm still often host to my children, and now my daughter-in-law, as we celebrate holidays, good news or simply a Sunday when we're all available. They are adults themselves now—in fact, I have asked them to contribute their perspectives on growing up in this book's conclusion.

Preparing our kids to face adulthood is not a job that starts when they're in grade twelve; it takes place thoughout their childhood. All along the way we are, in fact, raising our children to be capable adults. Whether it's how we encourage them to play, how we accommodate their particular temperament or what we do when they're squabbling, it's all part of the trip to maturity.

Parenting is a journey. In this book we'll talk about the trip you and your kids will make, from their first breath to their first apartment. It's an exciting trip, rich in experiences and joy. When they're young adults it may be the end of this book, but it's not the end of the journey. Your children grow and change (so do you!) and your relationship alters but doesn't diminish. The reason there's no word for adult children is that they remain our kids. Think about it: they're babies, toddlers, preschoolers, kids and teens and then they're adults, but still they're our children. And we never stop being a mom or dad.

Enjoy every step along the road as you give your kids their wings. I wish you a lifetime of happiness with your children.

CHAPTER 1

WHAT'S PLAY GOT TO DO WITH IT?

There are blocks of various shapes and sizes spread all over the living room floor. In the midst of this confusion sits eighteen-month-old Joey. He surveys his riches. It appears that the wealth of all these blocks is all he could want out of life. He takes one at random and places it on the floor; he then takes another and puts it on top. With glee he sweeps his hand across the stack and sends the two blocks flying. Then he picks them up and starts all over, only this time he uses four blocks. He continues this game, each time concentrating on building stacks of four, six and even eight blocks, then changing his demeanor as he joyfully reduces his stacks to rubble.

Eighteen-month-old Kendra is clapping her hands to the music. She's sitting on her mom's lap in a circle with six other toddlers and their parents at a play workshop at the local community center. She leans against her mother's chest, watching the other toddlers and imitating their behavior. At one end of the circle an upbeat leader directs the activity. During the songs, Kendra and her mom join the leader in the singing, and when the music stops they look to her for direction.

Are Joey and Kendra both playing?

The definitions of play vary from one expert to another, but they would all say that Joey is playing and Kendra is involved in a structured activity. It may be fun, but it's not play. This isn't to say that what Kendra and her mom are doing is a waste of time, but to look at play and its role in the development of independent and self-sufficient young adults, we first need to determine what constitutes play.

According to "The Play Video", produced by the Early Childhood Education program of Lethbridge Community College in Alberta, the definition isn't as important as the presence of certain qualities that characterize play.

Joey is playing. He's decided on his own to stack the blocks and then knock them down. It's not a game he was directed to play. He's in control of the play and has given some meaning to the building and destruction process. And in stacking, crashing, collecting and re-stacking the blocks, he's actively engaged in the play.

Play Includes the Following Features

- It's voluntary and intrinsically motivated.
- It's freely chosen.
- The child controls the activities.
- It's pleasurable, spontaneous and enjoyable.
- There's activity.
- There's a symbolic and meaningful component to the activity.

Kendra isn't playing. Her mother, the group leader and the other children are directing her in the activity.

You can look at play as a continuum from total play to no play, depending on the number of characteristics of a given activity. Joey is at the play end and Kendra is at, or very close to, the non-play end of the spectrum.

Why does it matter? And what does it have to do with raising children to be independent and self-sufficient?

While structured learning activities develop our skills, our learning is less internalized. When I read about a new activity, I may be able to imagine it but until I actually try it, it's just not going to be part of me. Even if I do understand, I need to draw on the experiences I have gleaned throughout my life to be able to imagine what the written instructions mean. Children don't have these experiences, so they need to develop their own. And play is the most effective way for them to learn.

Think about Joey. He's figuring out how to stack blocks so they remain stable, and he's learning what happens when he topples the pile. He's learning how to concentrate on a single activity, he's working on his hand/eye coordination, and he's making choices and developing his fine motor skills. Whew! How can so much learning be so much fun? This activity is giving him a base for eventually learning math, recognizing and comparing shapes, counting and understanding height and width.

He's also concentrating. We say that toddlers have short attention spans, and often they do, but when they're engaged in an activity that interests them, they can stick with it for longer than we ever imagined. Mind you, adults are the same. I can get into an activity I love and be astounded at how long I've been engaged, unaware of the passing of time.

Kendra is involved in her activity and certainly enjoying and benefiting from the closeness with her mom. The difference is that the adults have determined what the children will experience. When others direct most of our children's activities, kids do learn what's being presented but miss the chance to explore on their own and determine what they want to learn. They can develop skills but miss out on the passion. Exploring our interests and letting curiosity take the lead determine our passions.

We run the risk of making children's play so organized, supervised and academic that the value of play gets lost. Children have always played—because that's how they learn and grow. Play is the essence of childhood. And since it brings alive our curiosity, exploration and passion, play should continue throughout our lives.

That's play. In play we see children learning multiple skills and having fun doing so.

GAMES AND ACTIVITIES

We've all heard the line, "When I was a kid ... " and it sends us running. But stick with me. I was raised in the '50s, in the era of playing outside with all the other kids in the neighborhood all day long.

We played active games like tag and run-sheep-run, and games requiring dexterity like skipping and hopscotch. We played imaginative games like house and Cowboys and Indians (okay, not politically correct but it was the '50s!) and we played group games of baseball and Red Rover. And we did it all without an adult in sight. No coaches, no programs, no parents. We thought we were just having fun, but we were constantly testing ourselves, growing and developing skills and self-confidence.

THE DAY I WAS QUEEN

I made an entrance. I almost floated up the stairs and swept into the kitchen. I looked marvelous! I can't remember a time when I was so incredibly beautiful. Coming right behind me were my friends, and we all stood beaming as my mother welcomed us, complimented us on our fabulous outfits and served us tea and cookies.

We were eight years old. In actuality, our little size-three feet swam in the size-nine high heels we wore as we clumped up the basement stairs. Our dresses hung down off our shoulders and puddled on the floor, and the clunky jewelry we wore was at best over-done and at worst tacky.

And to this day, I remember the fun of reaching into the trunk full of Mom's cast-off clothing with my friends to put together our outfits, while creating stories of where we might be going. We were princesses and queens, we were society ladies and movie stars and we were our mothers going out for an important night on the town.

It was dress up play at its finest.

THEN AND NOW

When I think of children today and their hectic lives, I often recall times with my friend Sue. When we were young we'd often simply lie on the grass and stare up at the clouds. We'd talk about their shapes. "That one looks just like an alligator," I'd say just before a breeze came up, turning my alligator into pebbles.

Sue and I spent a lot of time interpreting clouds. We also climbed trees, had picnics in the park, swam in the river and captured snakes and frogs, which we tried to raise in boxes under her back porch.

We were creative, independent and resourceful. We got lots of fresh air and exercise, and had lots of time to do "nothing" and give our dreams space to emerge.

UNSTRUCTURED PLAY

Children thrive with a mix of structured and organized activities along with free play—play with no particular rules, goals or schedules. It's a time for children to be creative, imaginative and to dream.

Parents can foster this play by creating an environment that lets it happen. The first step and often the most difficult, is to let your children and their play spaces get messy. For example, on a rainy blustery day young children can create a world of excitement with a few blankets or sheets and permission to re-arrange the living room. Sheets over the furniture quickly become forts, ships at sea or a magic castle. Throw in some dress up clothes, and the children are set for the morning. At lunchtime you can serve lunch to your lords and ladies or to the sailors in the ship. Just throw a large beach towel on the floor and arrive with sandwiches and juice boxes. You can also eat with them and join in the fun.

Play that encourages flexibility is best for children. Allow your children free rein to decide how to play with their toys. Blocks can be anything from a fence around a play area, to a tower, to furniture for dolls.

School-age children often like to create longer-term activities. For example, they may take all their Lego people, cars and little buildings to create a town. For this they need a space that doesn't need daily pickup. This play is extremely valuable for children as they learn about using space, about re-arranging people and vehicles and about constructing buildings that don't fall down. Building a town is a long-term project, and giving our kids the opportunity to engage in this kind of play will allow them to stretch themselves, and to plan and execute complex projects. They'll get to problem-solve, to re-think some aspects and recover from mistakes and, in the end, see that all that work and thought is necessary and worthwhile.

When you provide a space for this kind of activity, you give a clear message of support.

WHAT ABOUT SAFETY?

"Can you recall a time when, as a child, you engaged in a potentially dangerous activity?"

When I asked that question of audiences in the '70s, all the men and most of the women had at least one example at their fingertips. In the '80s the numbers decreased until most women said no. In the '90s and the new century the numbers keep diminishing.

But taking risks is how children learn about their limits and their bodies. They need to test themselves. By pushing their limits, they're setting the parameters for themselves and learning to assess the level of their ability. I remember sitting on a park bench watching preschoolers on a climbing frame. The children who had parents within arm's length throughout the process would either hang back fearfully and try nothing or go too far, knowing that they had a safety net (mom or dad) right at hand. On the other hand, the children who were playing some distance from their parents were cautious, but challenged themselves to their limit.

Children need to test their limits, to discover the range of abilities their bodies offer. This testing is an important part of their physical development. Life isn't without risk, so our children need to learn how to handle themselves. When they're given appropriate freedom in their play from a very young age, they develop the capacity to assess risk and make healthy decisions throughout their lives.

I sometimes wonder whether the popularity of adventure holidays for adults in their 30s and 40s reflects having missed this chance in childhood. When I hear stories about road racing among teens, I have the same thought. This may be the first time they've had the chance to test themselves without an anxious parent in view. Over protected and oversupervised children have no idea how to judge risk, problem-solve or make good decisions when they're suddenly on their own.

ADULT ROLE IN CHILD PLAY

The role of adults is to facilitate play, not create it. We provide children with a great play environment and let them go to it.

A play environment doesn't need to be expensive. When my children were little, one of the favorite toys for all the kids in the neighborhood was an ancient, broken down hi-fi. This was an old television set, radio and record player all housed in one cabinet. We took the back off the cabinet, removed the glass picture tube and any other parts that were sharp or dangerous. There was a box of tools available to the kids, and for the better part of a year all the kids would gather to poke around the innards of this fascinating piece of electronic equipment.

My mother created a great play environment by simply putting all her cast-off clothing and shoes in a trunk and giving us free rein to dress up to our heart's content. The tea party at the end let us know that she sanctioned and applauded our play and that made it even more exciting. But at no point did she develop the rules or direct the activity.

When parents become directly involved in their children's play, they unintentionally inhibit their imaginative lives. Kendra isn't being creative or using her imagination, she's clapping when everyone else claps. So the learnings aren't the same as play. On the other hand, Kendra is having a nice time with her mom, learning to be part of a group and enjoying the music. Organized activities have their place in addition to play.

This isn't to say we shouldn't play with our kids. Good heavens, this is one of the true perks of having children! The trick is to play with your kids and let them set the pace and the activity. Our goal isn't to teach a lesson, although that may happen, but it's to join with our child in his play activity. You may simply watch, you may follow directions or you may suggest new wrinkles in the game.

How to Play with Your Children

Take a supporting role in your children's play. Let them take the lead and have fun.

- **Be present**. Simply make yourself available to your child. The child determines your activity level.
- **Accept an invitation to play**. If your child wants you to dance with her or join her finger-painting, say yes.
- **Support activities**. Provide a pail and shovel for your intrepid sandbox baby or suggest a picnic lunch in the tent he created from blankets and sheets.
- **Suggest options**. As you watch a play activity progress, you can bring a new idea to the piece: "What if you took the dolls for a walk in your wagon?"
- **Make child-friendly rules**. If you enjoy table games, change the rules to recognize your child's ability to level the playing field so that it's fun for all.
- **Relax and have fun**.

IN OTHER WORDS ...

- Play is the essence of childhood. If we want our kids to grow up to be self-sufficient and independent with good problem-solving skills, play is the place to start.
- Play isn't to be confused with organized recreation or simple physical activity like walking to school.
- Parents or other adults can support play by providing the opportunity and space for children to choose their activities.
- Kids need to experience a range of play activities, from physical play to creative and imaginative play.

Talking about Behavior
Kathy's Q & A

QUESTION

Help! My seven-year-old son thinks he's Nintendo-deprived. Although we've managed to stand firm so far and have no game system in our home, the pressure is intense. He seems to be the only kid around who doesn't have a system and he thinks we're just being mean about it. We're worried that if we get one, it will become a huge source of conflict. Are we being too restrictive?

ANSWER

These games are very popular with youngsters today. You need to ask yourself whether you're opposed to Nintendo or worried about the conflict it will cause. If you're opposed, then you simply state that you don't believe in the toy and why. Many parents have taken this kind of stand about war toys.

If, however, the potential conflict is the issue, then it's a different problem. In that case you may want to allow him to have the game but negotiate clear rules and limits as to the use. And, yes, this will lead to conflict. But learning to live within the time limits can be a good lesson for your son.

When the game is new I'd suggest you allow him extra playtime for the first weekend or week. It's a novelty and it's not unexpected that he'll want to play as much as possible. Let him know that he can have extra playtime for this initial period, then have him cut back to the already agreed upon limits.

You may also want to talk to his friends' parents about how they handle video game play.

Also, try it yourself. You may have fun, and your son will be thrilled to teach you.

QUESTION

My sixteen-month-old daughter is constantly pushing the boundaries of physical safety. She repeatedly climbs on the kitchen counter, jumps off the back of the sofa, dives down the slide. I can't seem to make her stop. What should I do?

ANSWER

All children need lots of large-muscle play. Those like your daughter need even more. Going to the local park or playground on a daily basis can help solve this problem. She needs to run, jump and roll in wide-open spaces as much as possible. Toddler gym programs are another good idea. Check out your local Y or community center to see what's available.

Providing these opportunities for her to exercise is only part of the solution. You also need to thoroughly childproof your home, and this means more than locks on the medicine cabinet and plug covers on electrical outlets. You may need to keep all the chairs in one room, and keep that room off limits with a gate or locked door. Cover the sharp edges of table corners and counters to prevent injury from the falls she's going to take. Use screws to fix climbable furniture like bookshelves to the wall. Rearrange the room to make the most dangerous furniture unavailable. Your interior design may not get the Martha Stewart seal of approval, but it will be toddler-friendly, and that's vital.

If your daredevil daughter is getting lots of physical exercise, is learning how to handle her body in a gym program and is living in a childproofed environment, she'll be safer and you'll be saner.

QUESTION

My nine-year-old son is an only child. I thought I was doing the right thing by playing with him all the time when he was little, but now he doesn't know how to play alone. He's in a panic unless he's got a string of playdates lined up. Please give me some guidance on how to break this pattern. I worry about his dependency on other kids and on us.

ANSWER

Some children find it easier to play alone than others. So it's not just that you helped him find people to play with, it could also be his personality.

Give him the responsibility for finding his own company. Are there children who live nearby for him to play with outside of a more formal setup? Hand him the task of filling his time. This gives him the choice to play with others or alone.

When your son is alone and complaining, resist the temptation to offer solutions. You can introduce him to some individual activities like solitaire. Also, make sure he has craft supplies, books and building toys to help him while away his solitary hours. Reassure him that you know he can find something to do, then go about your business. To wean him off his dependency on others, you can let him know that you're busy for the next half hour, then you can spend time with him.

Involve him sometimes in working with you rather than always playing. You get your work done, and he learns all kinds of useful skills. Children really like working with their parents.

CHAPTER 2

ONE SIZE DOES NOT FIT ALL

My son, Foley, was born. He was handed to me and as he lay in my arms, I realized that everything I'd been thinking for the past nine months was incorrect. He's my second child, and all through the pregnancy I told myself that knowing how to parent this child would be so much easier. After all, I'd done it before. Then I held him. And immediately I realized that this wasn't just another baby, but a unique human being totally unlike his sister.

When Foley's sister, Chelsea, was minutes old she'd curled up in my arms in a neat little package. Foley squirmed and wriggled. From the very beginning he wanted to be mobile. I held him with his head in the crook of my arm and his little bottom near my hand. I expected him to pull his arms and legs into his body, but he extended them. They hung over my arm waving madly. I had no idea what to do, but I certainly knew that this was a different baby from my first! So, I looked him in the eye and said, "Okay, I'll take care of your head and trunk. Your arms and legs are your problem."

Chelsea wanted to look at things, so we created a visual environment that kept her entertained. Foley fussed until by four months he was crawling and getting around on his own. For him, we had to create large and safe environments for him to explore.

I imagine if I'd had more children, I'd have discovered more differences. Each child is unique. One way to look at children's differences is to consider their temperament. Temperament determines how people view life. It's their basic character, their inborn disposition. And it's one reason why children from the same family can be so different. It's not the only reason. Birth order is another factor. My daughter, my first-born, came with her temperament into a household that had never had children. The second child was just that—second. His parents already had fourteen months of experience. We'll talk about birth order in more detail later in this chapter.

WHY TEMPERAMENT MATTERS

Taking a look at temperament is a good way to help you get to know your child. For that matter, you can also think about your spouse, friends and other family members, not to mention yourself. Understanding how we're alike and how we're different from the people we live and work with can help us interact more effectively. It's who we are but not how we behave. So once you've taken a look at your child and figured out what inborn traits are driving his responses, you can determine how best to help him move toward independence and self-reliance.

In my first book, *Who's In Charge Anyway?*, I talked about the importance of setting long-term goals so that we know what we want to teach our children as they grow. Knowing what drives them makes it easier for us to figure out how to help them learn what we want to teach them. It also helps us to reach our parenting goals. So, temperament is how your child reacts; his actions are how he behaves. Your job is to help him behave in positive ways. Temperament isn't an excuse to misbehave or to avoid learning how to become independent and self-reliant.

WORKING WITH TEMPERAMENTAL TRAITS

My son, Foley, rated high on activity level; he never stayed still. If I wanted him to pay attention, I first had to make sure that he got the exercise his body craved. We spent many hours at the park and found an excellent toddler and preschool gym program. We were also regular patrons at the local swimming pool. Do you

Temperament Traits: An Overview

Alexander Thomas and Stella Chess, pioneers in the study of temperament, identified as many as nine dimensions of temperament as they followed 136 children from toddlerhood to adult life. Each temperament trait exists in a continuum: for each of these nine traits there are people at the high end and on the low and everywhere in between. Let's look at the two extremes of each trait:

Activity Level

At one end is the high-energy kid who never stays still and craves physical activity. At the other end is the child who is quite sedentary and prefers "quiet" play. While you love watching your high-energy kid on the soccer field, the quieter child is a boon when you're going to visit Grandma.

Adaptability

Moving through the day—getting up, having breakfast, preparing to head out in the car—is a simple process if you have a highly adaptable child. She manages all the transitions in any day with confidence. At the other end of the scale is the child who needs predictability and a very slow orientation period to adjust to any change.

Approach/Withdrawal

Bring on new foods, new activities or new people—this child likes novelty. On the other hand is the cautious child who takes new situations extremely slowly. In many ways we worry less about the cautious child because she'll look carefully before jumping into a new situation, while her sibling just loves the variety and may not be too thoughtful before trying something new.

Distractibility

The distractible child can be easily diverted and may have trouble focusing. The other side of this coin is the child who concentrates so intensely, he doesn't even hear you calling!

Intensity

This child has strong emotions about *everything*, while her opposite is easygoing and undemonstrative. Our intense child will let us know how she feels, and it will often be over the top, while her calmer sister will sometimes seem neutral about everything.

Mood

Children have their own typical mood or outlook on life, ranging from the sunny disposition of the generally happy baby to the somber child with a serious approach to life.

Persistence

Our persistent child hangs in there in the face of all obstacles (including parents), while the child who is easily frustrated gives up quickly. We're proud of our persistent child when she's learning how to ride a bike, but when she wants a cookie right before dinner, we wish she could give up more easily!

Regularity

Some babies have a natural rhythm that brings regularity to their sleeping, eating and elimination, making their schedule very predictable. At the other end is the baby whose sleep and hunger are so erratic that he never settles a daily routine.

Sensitivity

The child who is physically sensitive is alert to (and affected by) all kinds of stimuli in her environment: scratchy socks, unpleasant smells and the beautiful colors in a sunset. Meanwhile, her counterpart at the other end of the scale may not even notice that she's put on her big sister's sock by mistake, and it's all scrunched up in her shoe.

On the emotional level is the child who is easily hurt by simple comments but is also very aware of other people's feelings. At the other end of the spectrum is the child who is resilient to others' remarks but may not notice when his friends are upset.

---

know that you can change a diaper from the south end of a toddler rapidly crawling north? If you do, you have a high activity child. I became an expert! I learned that he would fidget when talking to me and wriggle about in his chair. Making the accommodations to his needs led to a happy situation for all of us.

When Bradley wakes up in the morning or after naps, he isn't ready to face the world right away. When getting Bradley from his bed, Dad has learned to move slowly and doesn't immediately bring him into the light and activity in the rest of the house. He picks him up and talks softly until he feels Bradley relax, then he moves away from the bedroom. Bradley needs time to adjust to other transitions in his day, too. His parents have learned to maintain his routine, let him know what he can expect and always let him eat off his favorite plate.

Caitlin's mom was talking to some friends about her daughter's first day at preschool. Mom was anxious: how would her daughter handle this big step? Well, Caitlin barely looked back as she headed off to her new adventure. It was definitely harder on mom than daughter. It's a joy to watch Caitlin embrace life and see every new experience as a positive adventure. On the other hand, her parents need to watch her carefully because this very enthusiasm for new experiences can lead her to rush into danger.

Jeremy is easy to distract. When he's about to muck about in the big plant in the living room, his dad just shows him a toy on the other side of the room and Jeremy moves on. But Jeremy moves quickly from one activity to another, never staying with one thing for long. His dad makes sure there's a range of toys and activities available, so Jeremy can move from one thing to another without getting into trouble. He knows that arranging for lots of variety is worth the effort when he sees Jeremy playing easily and happily.

Isabelle is one passionate child. Her laugh is contagious; when she's excited and happy you can't help but smile. But Isabelle brings the same intensity to unhappiness, so her parents need to stay calm while she explodes with misery or joy. Living with Isabelle can be quite a roller-coaster ride. At first her parents would join in with her glee and suffer with her when she was unhappy. It was exhausting. They soon learned to look more objectively at Isabelle's moods. As Isabelle grew older, they started to teach her to more accurately assess the appropriate level of intensity. She'll never be a calm person, but with her parent's help she's learning to moderate her strong reactions, so she doesn't overwhelm other people or throw herself into despair over every little setback.

Shayla was learning how to ride a trike. She was determined to make it and simply wouldn't stop trying until she got it right. She fell off, brushed the grit from her knees and got right back on. She tried to pedal and her feet missed, so that the pedal swung aimlessly and her foot hovered, trying to find the pedal. Finally, she put it all together and happily took off up and down the driveway. Her persistence is admirable, and her parents are proud of her spunk, at least until she becomes just as determined to get at the CD player to see how it works. Shayla's parents need to develop persistence of their own, so that Shayla learns that the limits they set are firm.

Regularity is often something we crave from our children. Wouldn't it be wonderful to know exactly when they'll sleep, how much they'll eat for dinner and how they want to be comforted? My friend Marilyn had two children who napped at the same time every day. Both of them. But Marilyn's kids weren't very adaptable. Marilyn learned that while she could count on her kids' schedule, she needed to stick to it. If Marilyn wanted to change the routine, have a late dinner or get everyone up an hour earlier for a trip, she needed to plan it carefully so her kids could cope.

Tamara is very picky about what she eats; the texture of foods can drive her nuts. She's also sensitive about noises or any kind of discomfort. Her parents sometimes feel that she's just being too difficult. But it's real for her. She's bothered by many things and unless her parents learn to accommodate her, every action will be a fight. Her folks paid attention and identified the foods, clothing and noises that were most disturbing to Tamara. They not only tried to accommodate her as much as possible, they taught her what bugged her so, like a child with allergies, she could start to take control of her own environment.

Leo's uncle can tease him unmercifully, and it just rolls off Leo's back. Emotionally, he just isn't sensitive at all. Leo's uncle has realized, however, that Leo also doesn't recognize when others are hurting. He's so resilient he assumes everyone is just like him. So his uncle has started telling him stories about other people and how they feel so that Leo can be empathetic to those more sensitive than he.

These are some examples of parenting kids who have very distinct temperamental traits. Most of our children fit somewhere in the middle, but considering temperament will still make our parenting job simpler because we'll know what they need from us. Each person's temperament is the lens through which she sees the world. In a busy, active classroom a regular child may see chaos while a spontaneous child thrives. When we learn to look through the lens that defines our child's view of the world, we can more simply and effectively help him to attain the independence and self-sufficiency that is our ultimate parenting goal. I bet some of you, while reading this chapter, suddenly said, "Now, I get it! Now I see what's going on with my child." You're looking through her eyes and seeing the world as she sees it. Now you can reach her. Remember, a difficult temperament is no reason to give up on teaching your child. Rather, a child with a challenging temperament is going to need extra coaching and support to become a capable and competent adult.

TEMPERAMENTAL STYLES: THE SIMPLE VERSION

A broader but simpler way to look at temperament is to ask yourself whether your child has an *easy* style, a more *difficult* style or a *slow-to-warm-up* style. You probably noticed that the nine traits fit easily into one of these simple categories. If you have an *easy child*, you can simply get on with the task of raising her. She likely fits in the middle of most of the traits that we just discussed.

A *difficult child* needs a parent who will work with her to reach her goals. Start by changing the description. Although most may call her difficult, try saying, "Samantha is feisty." While she may try to defy your restrictions, she's also standing up for herself. So you want to teach her how and when to speak her mind without alienating everyone around her, including you. She'll need to learn, too, that while it's good to take a strong stand for what she believes in, it's also important to compromise, or even accept defeat gracefully. Role-play with her. "Samantha, instead of stamping your foot and yelling, what about if you said, 'I don't think we need to do that because …'" Instead of trying to elicit her agreement, hear her out when she objects to doing whatever you asked and then respond, "You don't have to like it, but you still have to do it." Whenever possible, celebrate the strengths of her challenging nature, and help her explore new ways to do things. For example, encourage her to join the debating team at school. What a great place for her to take a stand but at the same time defend her point of view. You can also remind yourself that she isn't likely to be a teen who mindlessly follows the crowd.

Slow-to-warm-up children can be a real challenge because we want to protect them from this life that seems to hold so many fears for them. Instead of sheltering them from reality, though, we need to learn to move more slowly. The expectations and goals remain the same. For example, it's good manners to greet guests coming into your home by saying hello and shaking hands. With the easy child, you simply have to show him what you expect and odds are he'll cooperate. The difficult child may have trouble adjusting to the task or want to decide whom she will or will not greet. You need to work with her to let her know that simple courtesy is expected. She doesn't have to like a person to be polite. With your slow-to-warm-up child, you need to break the task down into smaller components. So first, four-year-old Morgan may simply have to be with you holding your hand. The next time (or a few weeks later), he's able to say hello but can maintain the safety of holding onto you. The first time he's expected to shake hands may be with someone he knows well. The final outcome is the same for all three, but the process changes.

Another way to look at temperament is to see if your child is an *introvert* or an *extrovert*. An extrovert is usually described as a "people person." She gets her energy from being with people, so she loves parties and social events. An introvert can enjoy being with friends, but he also finds it draining. He gets his energy from solitude. Approximately three-quarters of people are extroverts so odds are you and your children are extroverted at least to some extent. But an extroverted parent with an introverted child can have problems understanding why she wants to spend so much time alone. In Chapter Three, we talk about Sonja, who didn't have a big group of friends. Once her parents accepted that she's an introvert and not lonely or unhappy, they were able to accept her "alone time" as healthy for her.

BIRTH ORDER

The culture surrounding your child also has an impact, and birth order is one factor worth looking at. Psychologists who follow the teachings of Alfred Adler have developed a description of typical characteristics of people based on their position in the family. Like the temperamental traits, this is simply a tool. It's a lens through which you can view yourself and your kids and see if it helps your understanding of what makes your child tick. It would be nice if we could simply place children on a continuum of temperamental traits, consider their birth order and whether they're introverts or extroverts, and develop a plan guaranteed in twenty years to produce an independent, capable young adult with high self-esteem. Wow, if that were the case imagine the book I could write! But people are more complex than that. Nothing is absolute, but the more you can understand your

Birth Order Characteristics

These are some characteristics seen as typical of people based on their position in the family:

Only child

Because she's the only child, and her parents spend a great deal of time talking to her, she's likely to be articulate and may relate more easily to adults than to her peers. When there are more than five years between children, each often resembles an only child.

Oldest

First-borns are known for being responsible high achievers and can be authoritarian. Depending on the number of children, they may be called on to look after younger siblings. If they feel that the amount of care-giving they provide is unfair, they can resent the other kids. On the other hand, if they believe the requests are reasonable, their responsible ways flourish.

Second-born

The second-born is often the opposite of the first-born in terms of interests. I believe this is because she's trying to find her place in the family and finds her uniqueness in being different from her older sibling. Today, the second child is very often also the youngest. She can become competitive with the older child.

Middle child

Today, with smaller families, there are fewer middle children. Sitting between other children, looking up to the older and down to the younger, they often become good mediators and peacemakers. They're flexible, learning how to adjust to be accepted by the older and get along with the younger.

Youngest

The youngest soon learns to be charming and cute in order to get his way. Last-borns are often fun and usually outgoing. The parents know this is the last child and enjoy him; and the older kids are often surrogate parents. The youngest child may never seem to grow up because the family wants him to stay the baby.

child's unique way of understanding the world, the easier it is for you to do your job. I'm an oldest, and my sense of responsibility has always been intense. I take life pretty seriously. My next sister, in true birth order fashion, is the opposite. She's fun-loving and bubbly. Our middle sister is the peacemaker. She works to maintain a balance among us, and the youngest, what do you know, is cute and charming. Of course, it's not that simple. My sisters and I are more complex than this simple description would suggest. I can have fun; the second takes her work very seriously, the middle has the strength of her convictions and won't back down from them, and the youngest also focuses on her responsibilities. In addition to our place in the family, we each have our own individual temperaments, and our culture and environment also played a role in shaping us.

When we were children, our parents died and we went to live with relatives who adopted us. They had two children, a classic responsible one and a charming youngest. On top of that, they were boys. Interestingly, we continued to maintain the basic characteristics in this new relationship. There were a female oldest and a male oldest as well as a male youngest and a female youngest. The gender differences played a role in our ability to maintain our positions without competition.

IN OTHER WORDS ...
- Every child is unique.
- Temperament and birth order are two tools we can use to help us understand each of our children. The better we know our children, the better job we can do of raising them to mature adulthood.
- These are tools, not excuses for avoiding the responsibility of parenting.

TALKING ABOUT BEHAVIOR
Kathy's Q & A

QUESTION
I didn't realize my four-and-a-half-year-old was so shy until he started playschool this year. When the teacher asks a question, most

of the other kids' hands pop up, but not my son's. I'm concerned about the missed opportunities. How can I help him overcome his shyness?

ANSWER

If he were truly shy you'd probably have noticed it by now. By his age he's had many other opportunities to interact with both children and adults. However, if this is the first time he's been part of a bigger group, he may simply be a bit overwhelmed and need some time to get comfortable. Some of his classmates are probably experienced through daycare or other group activities. If this is the case, just give him the time he needs. Different people learn in different ways and at different speeds. Your son may be the kind of person who likes to listen and take in material without actively participating. When he's telling you about his time at playschool, if he talks about what the teacher said, then he's participating in his way. You may also wish to talk to the teacher about your concerns. It may be that he approaches her at other times and asks his questions one-on-one. Does he seem to enjoy himself? Is he happy to be at playschool? Does he have at least one friend in the group? If the answers are yes, relax and let him be who he is.

QUESTION

My six-year-old has just started grade one, and she seems to have picked up this "bad girl" attitude. She's not disrespectful to her mom or me, it just seems that she's taken control of how she dresses, what she eats, et cetera. My wife refers to it as confidence. I'd like to know if this is a mild case of peer pressure, or is my little girl growing up and becoming part of the gang?

ANSWER

Although you mention a "bad girl" attitude, I don't see an example of negative behavior, just a wish to have more control over her choices. As long her choice of clothing or food fits with the family expectations or values then this is a step to be celebrated. It's often hard to see our children move toward independence, but it's healthy and natural. Our job is to monitor their activity and set limits and boundaries that are age-appropriate. Since she's interested in her diet, you'll want to get her more involved in menu planning, grocery shopping and meal preparation. This is a great opportunity to teach her about nutrition and have her learn to cook. She can then prepare some of the foods she likes for the whole family.

The same applies to her interest in clothing. Let her shop with you and make choices within your budget. You can help her learn how to choose different styles for different occasions.

QUESTION

Adam, my eight-year-old son, is a real homebody. Although he plays hockey once a week and takes piano, he's not interested in other activities. I feel this is the age when he should be exposed to a lot of different activities at an introductory level, so he can then discover his passions. There are things I think he'd enjoy and be great at, but I'm reluctant to push. What's the best approach here?

ANSWER

I suggest you follow Adam's lead. He has chosen two different healthy activities: hockey provides physical exercise, team co-operation and socialization; piano offers mental exercise, personal discipline and solitary work. Both activities supply lots of structure and challenge. I generally suggest to parents that two extracurricular activities in addition to school is plenty for kids. School and homework are tiring and time-consuming, and kids who take on too many activities can easily burn out. As well, spending time at home is beneficial. This gives him time to dream, read and simply hang out with other family members. Appreciate that he wants to be with you and that he enjoys your company and can also enjoy his own company.

It's a good idea for children to be involved in some extracurricular activities throughout childhood and, you're right, this does give them the chance to sample different things. But there are many ways for him to gain exposure to other sports or hobbies. He's probably trying out new sports in gym class at school, and he likely talks to friends about their activities. He'll try new things when he's ready. As long as he's happy and healthy, I wouldn't worry. He's doing what he wants to do for now, and that's just fine.

CHAPTER 3

WHAT ARE FRIENDS FOR?

It was a lovely summer day. My mother and I were standing under the rose arbor at the side of our new home. I was in front of her, leaning against her legs. We were facing another mother and daughter combo, and the two adults were grinning delightedly. The talk had started with the neighbor welcoming us to the neighborhood and ended with the two women deciding that as their daughters, Sue and I, were only six months apart in age we should become friends. We were four and five years old at the time. For young children, friendships are more about proximity than shared interests. They end up playing with the children of their parents' friends, with neighbor kids or with the other children at daycare. But once they're in elementary school, particularly by grade one or two, they start to look for children who share their interests.

Six-year-old Kayla and her mom, Denise, went to the park at the end of the street. It's a wonderful area with imaginative climbing equipment, a big sandbox and a large field. Kayla kept bugging her mom to join her in the play, but Denise wasn't interested in rolling down the hill or swinging from her knees on the climbing frame. So Kayla wandered around listlessly, half-heartedly swinging on the swing or digging a bit in the sand. Then along came Gary and his daughter, Regina, and Kayla brightened right up. Her friend Regina is also six, and soon the two girls were having a great time together. The park alone isn't enough for them anymore; they want the social connection with someone who shares their interests. Over time the girls learned how to decide what to play next and how to share. They developed games with rules and expectations. And they learned how to walk to the park on their own.

Friendships play an integral role in developing independence. It sounds like an oxymoron, as we tend to equate independence with managing alone, and yet here I'm saying it's about your child's relationships with peers. For children, independence is about separating from their parents and getting on with their lives as part of their own generation. Separation starts with their first independent breath, and continues throughout childhood. Friendships further that process. Separation from parents doesn't mean abandoning that primary and important relationship. It means being able to function in a mature way in the world as their own person. One person who has achieved a healthy separation from her parents knows her own mind, makes mature decisions and has healthy relationships with friends, peers, colleagues and family.

THE TICKLISH TASK OF MAKING FRIENDS

I remember once when my nephew, Richard, came to visit. He was six at the time and an only child. He headed outside, found another child about his age and with confidence said, "I'm Richard, will you be my friend?" His parents never had to worry about him making friends. It's not as easy for all children.

Reagan, for example, goes outside at recess and stands watching the other kids play. Because no one approaches her, she figures they just don't like her, so she withdraws more and more into herself. From their conversations her mom knows this is happening. She could talk to Reagan's teacher to get her support. The teacher could suggest to the other kids that Reagan would like to play. They'd probably be happy to include her; they just didn't know she was interested. Later, Reagan's mom could talk to her about how to join in the schoolyard games. She can role-play with her, teaching her to say, "Hi, can I join in?" Today, we don't feel comfortable letting a child simply head out on the street or to the park in search of other kids. Instead, Reagan's mom could ask the teacher if there's a particular child Reagan would enjoy playing with. She could then encourage Reagan to invite the child over when they're going somewhere like the swimming pool or zoo. If there's a child the same age on their street, she could also sound out the mother about going for a walk or other outing together, or simply invite mom and child over one afternoon. She could make sure there's something concrete for the kids to do, so their first meeting isn't awkward. Once kids know at least one other child in the neighborhood, they can start to play and will likely be joined by other pairs or groups of children.

In her after-school program, Sonja sits alone at the edge of the field watching a butterfly on the flowers. She's absorbed in her activity and happy to be alone. At first her parents were concerned by her lack of friends. They kept encouraging her to join the kids' games and pushed her to participate. Finally, after talking to her, they realized that she's quite happy as she is. She has a good friend in her pottery class and that's enough for her. Once her parents respected her need for some alone time, they noticed that when Sonja wanted to play with other children she was quite comfortable joining the group.

PLANNING PLAY

Friends play an important role in your child's development. Playing with other kids teaches them to share, take turns, negotiate, and bow to the wishes of the group in order to stay involved. Ten children ranging in age from eight to ten were at the park. A few parents were also there, enjoying a chat and resting on the benches. The group of youngsters decided to get a game going. It was like soccer but not exactly: the rules had to take into account some small trees on the field. They debated about whether to have five kids or fewer on each team, so they could take turns. Then they needed to determine which kids would be on which team. If team one got Riley, who was an awesome goalie, team two wanted Kendra who was an incredible forward. Time passed. The parents got restless. If these kids didn't hurry up and play there'd be no time. Why couldn't they get on with it?

Many of us can relate to that. Kids can spend forever determining the rules for a game. Whether it's a team sport, a craft activity or imaginative play they organize and negotiate at length. It drives us nuts. But it's what they need to do. Being with friends, whether it's one or twenty, teaches kids about cooperating with others, developing strategies to reach a goal (like developing a game for the group to play together) and being fair. The process is as important as the actual activity, maybe more so. This play, or specifically the planning, is a vital step to the world of negotiation, teamwork and problem-solving. So relax. If you can see the planning as an integral part of the activity, you won't go nuts watching them strategize instead of getting to the task at hand. If they never get to play the planned games, it's just fine.

FRIENDSHIPS VARY

Friendships and friends are as varied as the people involved in the relationship. At the start of this chapter, I mentioned meeting Sue. At first we were two little girls of about the same age, thrown together by geography. Over the next ten years, until I moved away, we were best friends. As young kids, this meant we spent much of our free time together playing in the bush and swimming in the river. It also meant that when I got really cold after swimming she'd wrap me in both my towel and hers, to help keep me warm. She didn't get cold. She was my best friend and looked after me.

As we got older we shared secrets and dreams. We'd go into the bush, build a campfire and sit and talk. Often Sue and I would join up with the other kids in the neighborhood. We learned that we needed to spend time together and to participate in the larger world. I moved away when I was a teen, but we never lost touch. The bond is too great to break easily. The intensity of a best friend is the base for developing intimacy with others, eventually a life partner. Best friends teach us about trust, and about becoming independent because we have the support of our best friend, who will be with us every step of the way. Best friends can be mirrors against which children reflect their ideas, their hopes and wishes, and test their goals for the future. Have you ever watched a group of eleven-and twelve-year-old boys play a role-play game? It's complex and intense. And it's important. When children get involved in an intricate game or project, they're learning how to work together to reach a goal. So as you watch them and think, "My goodness, aren't they taking this all a little too seriously?" remember that in ten years they could be bringing the same intensity to major health research.

Helping Your Child Make Friends at School

Beyond the neighborhood there's school; many kids meet and make friends at school. After all, that's where they spend a great deal of their time.

If your child seems lonely at school try the following strategies:

- Recruit the teacher. Ask if there's another child who might make a good match with yours. Then ask the teacher to pair them up for an activity.
- Role-play approaches. Teach her to walk up to kids with a smile and say, "Hi, can I play?"
- Encourage him to have one friend over, and take them on an outing so the social expectations are simple.
- Observe your child to discover whether he's doing anything to repel other kids. Is he being bossy or a bully?
- Get her involved in an activity she loves during which she can meet other kids with the same interest. It may be that the mix of kids at school just isn't suited to your child.
- Be a driver. Share carpooling to soccer practice with another parent so that your child is in the car with another child or two, with something in common to talk about.
- Understand that some kids have one or two close friends and are happy. Others want lots of kids around.

THE FRIEND FROM HELL

For weeks now, all Darren has talked about is Max, the new kid in his class. On Saturday Max came over to play. He came into the house and without even looking at you, grabbed Darren and ran down the hall. Soon you could hear them whispering and giggling from his bedroom. When you went in to say hello, Max looked at you as if you had two heads, and Darren rudely said that they were playing and to leave them alone. During lunch Max shoveled food into his mouth, talking all the while and kicking Darren under the table. After he left, you found that they had gotten into some important papers in the den. What do you do now?

Darren idolizes this little ruffian. The trick is to avoid criticizing Max. If you do, Darren will have to defend his new friend. Instead, focus on Darren's behavior. Talk to him about what happened during the visit, which house rules Darren broke, and let him know that the way he behaved when his friend was over was unacceptable. The next time Max comes over, meet him at the door and let him know what the house rules are. It may be that everything that drives you nuts about him is perfectly acceptable in his home. Tell him that in your home, you expect children to be polite so when he arrives he should come and say hello to you. Tell him what parts of the house are off-limits. Then, during the visit, deal with any transgressions as they occur. You can tell the boys that if they break the rules, Max will have to go home, and they can try again tomorrow. You may find that Max settles down at your place and is actually a nice kid. Or Darren may find that being in trouble every time he plays with Max simply isn't worth the grief.

Most kids show up at some time with a friend we just don't like. Suddenly we see Darren through new eyes. Is this the way he wants to be? Hasn't he paid any attention to what we've been teaching him? What's he thinking? Take a deep breath. Remember the cool but "bad" kid you knew as a child? Darren may simply be curious. He's never met a kid like this before and wants to explore the relationship. Or he may recognize that Max is hurting and needs a friend. Whatever it is, learning about different kinds of kids is healthy for your child. He's beginning to understand that not everyone is like him and his family. He's developing skills of tolerance and awareness, both important to his growing independence.

Occasionally, a child will meet and become entranced with a new friend who's truly a bad influence. You'll see your child's behavior deteriorate. Use the same tactics but more strongly. You can tell Darren that he simply can't be with the new friend because his behavior changes every time he's with him. Let your child take responsibility for only his own behavior and choices.

After all, the other child isn't making your kid change, but he sure is influencing him. When the change is truly serious, take your child for counseling so that you can determine if there's something that's causing your child to need to hook up with the bad news kid. With younger kids this could show up as a significant increase in tantrums, unusual levels of aggression or meanness towards pets. As they get older, signs of drug use, staying out all night or a sudden drop in marks are the signals that there's something more serious involved than simply wanting to experience a different sort of friend.

TEEN PEER PRESSURE

Marjorie has two teenage children. They're fabulous kids. Celine, the oldest, is involved in a marching band. Marjorie is thrilled. Celine isn't getting only an opportunity to enjoy and improve her music, she's getting regular exercise from the marching and has met some truly spectacular kids. Her younger daughter, Nicole, plays soccer and loves it. She's also making some great friends and getting exercise. Marjorie laughs when other parents worry about teens and peer pressure. Why, she wonders, do we always assume it's negative? One of Celine's friends introduced her to the band, and Nicole started soccer because one of the other kids wanted her to join.

Adolescence is a time to try new things, and having friends to experiment with makes it easier and more fun. And sure, not all the activities they try are the best. But the more we've helped them learn how to problem-solve and think through their decisions, the more likely it is that they'll make sensible choices. And when they do blow it (and they will, being, after all, human) they'll know how to take responsibility for their choices, recover and learn from their mistakes.

Peers do increase in importance to our children as they age. But that doesn't undermine their relationship with us. It does reduce the amount of time they spend with us. From the safety of home and family, teens reach out into the greater world as part of the process of becoming ready to leave home and be independent. They measure all their experiences against the teachings of home. So what looks like rebellion is usually simply assessment. How do my parents values and lifestyle choices stack up against those of my friends and their families? The trick here is balance, and boy, is it tricky!

It's also important to note that although teens do want to spend more time with their peers, it doesn't mean that they can or should avoid us. Family dinners, special events and holidays are examples of times we will ask them to join in. They may grouse and complain but don't pay any attention. Remember when they were toddlers and said, "No" with absolute authority, but then went on to participate happily in the family activity? Teens aren't unlike their toddler selves. The importance of family is a lesson they need to integrate so that they know that family is forever and that separation and independence doesn't mean the loss of family.

WHAT'S WRONG WITH THIS PICTURE?

Melinda and Justine pile out of the car in front of the café. They're obviously great friends who enjoy each other's company. It's Sunday morning, and after their coffee and pastry they settle down for a good gossip about their dates last night. Harold and Tyler are also in the café grabbing a quick coffee before they head off for a round of golf. Both pairs of best friends spend a great deal of time together. How wonderful! Or is it? You see, Melinda is Justine's mother and Harold is Tyler's father.

Melinda is also a single parent so sees herself and her daughter as members of the same dating scene.

While it's great to see parents and children enjoying each other and spending time together, is it healthy for them to be best friends? In a word, no. Justine and Tyler are both teens, who need teen friends. Their best friends should be their peers, not their parents. And Melinda and Harold, both in their early forties, also need to develop friendships among people their own age. What's going on here?

The TV show "The Gilmore Girls" celebrates the relationship of thirty-something Lorelei and her teenage daughter Rory. The show description says that they grew up together. How lovely. Then who parented young Rory while her mother was busy growing up? Children need parenting, which is an adult job. It takes a grown-up to raise a child. In our youth-obsessed society, many adults want to stay young and hip. How better to do that than become best friends with a sixteen-year-old? But hanging out with people less than half your age exacerbates the age difference. Two best friends, one with a tight pert body, the other a victim of gravity. How can the older friend compete? More importantly, who does the teen turn to when she needs help, advice and reassurance? If a teen sees her mom as a peer she won't see her as a resource, so may turn instead to a friend for help when she needs it. After all, she may see little difference between her teen friends and her mom, the middle-aged teenager.

Do we want our sixteen-year-olds to be parenting each other, or would we like them to come to us? If so, we need to be the mature adult in the relationship. Parenting is a special and unique role. Anyone can potentially be our friend; only our offspring can be our children. We should celebrate and honor this relationship. No matter what their age, our children will always be our kids. As they mature we'll find ourselves engaging in more friend-type activities, but at the end of the day, they're still our children. Our teens, in particular, need us to maintain our parent role. Adolescence is a challenging stage of development and requires the steady support and guidance of a caring and mature adult. Be friendly with your kids. Spend time with them. By all means, enjoy a round of golf or a double latté together. But be their parent, not their best friend. They'll thank you for it.

FRIENDS AND INDEPENDENCE

In the chapter on play we talked about the important lessons children learn through play. These lessons serve them well as they move toward independence. Friendship gives our kids the chance to pursue this learning with their peers. We say "our children are our future" and, hokey as that sounds, it's also true. They're the next generation, and they need to learn how to work together to make the world strong and healthy. With their friends, kids share experiences from their perspective, learn to develop and maintain relationships and learn how to choose people who share their interests and values. When you support your children's friendships you're helping them to become the strong adults we wish all our kids to become.

IN OTHER WORDS ...

- Friendships are vital to the development of an independent, capable young adult.
- Their relationships with other kids teach children about negotiation, sharing, teamwork and cooperation.
- Best friends teach kids about trust and intimacy.
- Peer pressure can be a good thing.
- Friends give children the security to try new things. It's easier to join band or take the bus downtown with a friend than to do it all alone.
- Children need parents to parent and peers to be friends.

TALKING ABOUT BEHAVIOR
Kathy's Q & A

QUESTION

My family recently moved and my seven-year-old daughter is having trouble making new friends. It's summer, so there isn't the immediate social network of school, and she's very lonely. How can I help her get over her shyness and, without being too intrusive, help her make some friends?

ANSWER

It's very difficult for kids to move in the summer. What you want to do is discover what activities attract the kids in your new neighborhood. The local community center or library are good places to start. Are there day camps or swimming lessons that she can join right away? Head over to the local park. Often there's a youth worker or park attendant arranging activities for the kids. This is a great way for her to meet local children. Talk to your new neighbors or ask coworkers about summer activities for kids. You may find that a colleague right down the hall has a youngster who can introduce your daughter to the neighborhood.

QUESTION

When daughter Sandy, eight, has a certain friend over, they go straight to her room, whispering and giggling. If my five-year-old son Jason wants to join them, they send him away. It's all very unpleasant. How can I convince Sandy to change friends?

ANSWER

A new friend isn't going to solve this problem. Most eight-year-old girls giggle and whisper with their friends and certainly don't want to be bothered with a little brother. I'd start by explaining to Sandy that going straight to her room without saying hello is bad manners. Let her know that you expect her and her friends to come in and say hi and chat for a moment. Then they may excuse themselves and go off to her room. This is a great opportunity for you and Jason to have some time together. Have him help you cook dinner or weed the garden so that the time is special for him.

At the same time, you need to be clear with Sandy that while they don't have to play with Jason, having a friend over doesn't give her permission to be mean or insulting. When you know that Sandy is going to have a friend over, you could arrange for Jason also to have a visitor. It's a good idea to invite your children's friends for dinner to give you a chance to get to know them better. When you make your home welcoming to your children and their friends, you generally discover that they're nice children, just like yours.

QUESTION

My six-year-old son has formed the habit of phoning friends to ask if he can go play at their houses. I keep telling him the proper thing to do is to either ask friends over to our house or wait for an invitation to a friend's house. I'm embarrassed by his constantly inviting himself over to other people's houses.

ANSWER

The first question is, does he ask his friends to come to your place to play? If he doesn't, you need to find out why. Do you allow them to make noise or make a mess? These are pretty basic components to the play of most six-year-olds. Kids choose where they want to play based on where they feel most comfortable and welcome. It's great if your house is the one all the kids love because you get to know all the children. As they get older, they'll continue to see your home as the place to be, and you'll know where your teenagers are and who they're with. On the other hand, among young children, inviting themselves to each other's houses is pretty typical and not seen as particularly rude. They don't understand why adults feel awkward about it. I imagine your son enjoys exploring the other children's rooms and toys, but he probably doesn't really care that much where they play. As he gets a bit older, he'll learn to ask first if his friend would like to play and then to work out together at whose house to meet.

CHAPTER 4

STOP IT, YOU TWO!

"Mom, she's got her hand on my side."

"No, my side ends here. You're hogging more than half of the seat."

"Stop it, you two!

Ever been there? If you have more than one child, this scenario will be familiar. Whether they're squabbling over toys or television shows or the back seat of the car, some days the squabbling seems constant. This wasn't the plan when you decided to have more than one child. Your vision was kids who played together, helped each other and were each other's best friend.

I have a photo of my kids when they were five and six years old. They're walking away arm in arm, heading off to play soccer, both in white shorts and yellow T-shirts. It's a lovely photo. And that's what we want for our kids all the time.

The reality is different. They disagree, they bicker, they argue, and they get along. Problem is, we tend to notice when they're being annoying, not when they're having a great time together. I'm so idealistic about sibling relationships that I have been known to whitewash the past. I simply refuse to remember the squabbles my children engaged in during their childhood. But then they start telling stories, the ones that start with "remember the time …" and I have to acknowledge that, yes, we sure had our moments.

So what does this have to do with helping kids to become independent and self-sufficient? Well, believe it or not, both the bickering and the getting along are all part of learning problem-solving, getting along with others, self-assertion and team-building.

So the next time they start to bicker you can smugly say to yourself, "Hey, they're developing all kinds of helpful life skills." Then you can yell, "Stop it, you two!' Or is that the only response we can make? Of course not. But first let's take a look at why they're fighting. What's going on here anyway?

"MOOOOOM, DAAAAAD!!! MAKE HIM STOP!"

You're trying to get dinner ready, but the calls from the next room keep interrupting. They can't seem to get along for five minutes without calling you in to help with some calamity or other. Every time you attempt to determine who started it, and try helping them to come up with a solution, you get nowhere. Why? Because you miss the real issue. Having you come in and try vainly to either problem-solve or act as judge, jury and executioner is the point. Yep. You're the entertainment this afternoon. Think about it. It doesn't matter what they're fighting over; they call you almost immediately. They're after your attention. If they didn't want you, they wouldn't invite you into the fray. So what do you do?

Some would say simply ignore them and let them figure it out. I have a problem with that, because odds are you've always shown up when called, so they have a right to expect that you'll continue to do so. If you suddenly stop, they may in fact hurt each other as they haven't learned to control their tempers. They have always had you to stop them before it gets serious. It's a learning process. Show up, but refuse to play the game. Don't behave in your usual manner. Be calm. Offer choices: "I have the TV remote. When you decide what you want to watch, come and tell me. Meanwhile, you can stay here and talk about it or you can come and help me in the kitchen." Help in the kitchen? You have to be kidding! I know, you're just trying to get dinner ready and having "help" isn't always helpful. But face it, they're interrupting you anyway. They want to spend time with you, and learning how to cook isn't a bad thing. So this is step one. Then you need to wean them off you.

Sit down with them at a quiet time and start helping them figure out some ways they can negotiate their own solutions. In time, they'll learn that there are better ways to get your attention and that, usually, they can work out their problems on their own. When a solution eludes them, they can come and talk to you or put the issue on the agenda for the next family meeting (see my book, *Who's In Charge Anyway?* for tips on running family meetings).

RIGHTEOUS RITA

Then there's everyone's favorite child. She stands in front of you with her halo glowing. Okay, not a real halo, but it still seems to be present. She looks so righteous you can hardly stand it. She doesn't want to have to do this, but for the good of the group, the neighborhood, maybe even the world, she must. She has to tell you what's happening. This is the tattler. She can't get her own way in the group on her own so she's coming to the source of all power, the closest available adult, to see if she can get some help.

With some tattlers you can simply tell them that you don't listen to tattling and that's that. They've learned that some adults listen and some don't. The tattler who perseveres is another story. Forget everything you know about good communication skills. Usually you stop what you're doing, turn to the child, make eye contact and get down to their level. Not in this case! Keep doing whatever you're doing and let her talk. Nothing will stop this child. When she's done, say something like, "I'm sure you can work it out." She'll soon learn that expecting others to handle her problems isn't the solution, and she'll figure out ways to problem-solve on her own.

What about those times when they come to tell you something serious? There's a difference between tattling and telling. Typically, while the tattler arrives looking self-righteous, a child who is coming to tell looks frightened or worried. Something is out of control, and she needs your help. It can be a toddler climbing to unsafe heights, a child about to handle tools or a teenager who has had too much to drink and is about to try driving a car. If you're unsure, check it out. It's better to be safe than sorry.

Learning to recognize the difference is a process. When we refuse to get involved with a tattler but do respond quickly when our children need help, we teach them the difference. They then learn that it's the responsible thing to get help when the situation is out of control. When they're teens, telling can be tough because they may be seen as snitches, but if the safety or life of another teen is in jeopardy, it's the right thing to do. When they become adults, we use the term whistle-blower for a person who has the courage to publicize a clearly wrong action and, like teens, these adults are often castigated. But they're doing the right thing.

THE AGE GAP

Donna was at her wits' end with her two children, four-year-old Max and his little sister, Eileen, fourteen months. Whenever they were left alone, Eileen would be crying within minutes, and her mom would have to come and get her. Donna couldn't understand why Max was so mean to his sister. One day, Donna stood just outside the playroom door to watch what was happening. Max went to the far corner of the room and picked up a toy; Eileen looked around, opened her mouth and started to howl. Max was nowhere near. It turned out that the first time Max tried to play with his sister, he tossed a ball that hit Eileen, and she fell over and started to cry. Max was confused: that's how he plays with other kids. So from then on he simply avoided her. Eileen, on the other hand, learned that crying as soon as Max was in the room led to attention from her mom. It had simply become a habit.

Preschoolers don't know how to play with babies; they need to be shown. Donna started playing with the two kids together, all the time talking to Max about what he could do to have fun with his sister without hurting her. Soon they could play happily. Now that Eileen is a bit older, there's a new challenge: she drives her brother nuts by getting into his "big boy toys" like Lego and messing up his projects. Of course, these little toys are also dangerous for her. Max doesn't want to be relegated to playing alone in his room. One family I know solved the problem by having the older child play in the playpen! He could be in the room, the baby could see him but not get at his stuff, and everyone was happy.

Then there's the day one child becomes a teen. It doesn't matter what the age spread is. When one is a teen and the sibling is, according to the teenager, a "dumb little kid," there's tension. Sometimes this just takes time; once the younger is also a teen the tension lifts. But meanwhile your teen needs to be reminded about the family rules concerning civility. It's not okay to insult or put down another family member. The logical consequence is that he removes himself until he can, at minimum, be polite. Mind you, the younger child also needs to know that "Nah, nah, nah" isn't an acceptable response when his teenage sibling is being reprimanded. And a certain amount of verbal sparring (okay, it's worse than that) is likely to go on. If it's a two-way match, you can tell them that you don't want to listen to them and that they should take it outside. One time when I spoke to my kids about their teasing, they said, "It's our relationship and we're okay." So I just told them I didn't want to hear it. Today they're best friends.

JOINT PROJECTS

Four-year-old Maddy and six-year-old Jake decided they wanted to have a tent in the living room. They got a sheet from their mom and set to work. For the next hour they experimented with where to put it. They tried out the sheet over the couch, then over some chairs and finally over a table. That worked best, and they crawled into their new and private world and began planning what they'd do there and what toys they'd bring to their great new space.

Twelve-year-old Emma and her thirteen-year-old brother Nathan decided that it would be cool to have a skating rink in the backyard. There was a good flat space, a pile of snow and cold temperatures. So they talked to their dad, who told them exactly what they'd have to do. All weekend they worked together in the yard to prepare the surface for the rink, and on Sunday night Dad inspected the work, declared it a success and they began flooding the area. By the following weekend they were skating on their rink.

Working together to make something happen is a great skill and one that many siblings manage well. Our job is to get out of the way and let them do it. Be available as a resource when needed, but if we want our kids to learn how to look after themselves, we need to give them opportunities throughout their childhood to practise. Children can gain this valuable experience only by working on joint projects with their friends. You can help by providing the space and materials to support their big ideas.

WHAT ABOUT BABYSITTING?

When Amy turned twelve, she took the babysitting course offered by the Red Cross. She loved the course and immediately got the word out through the neighborhood that she was ready to look after children. There was only one family she wasn't keen on babysitting—her own. She really didn't enjoy looking after her two younger brothers and resented the fact that she didn't get paid for this work.

Being the oldest child in a family carries with it certain privileges and responsibilities. Looking after the younger kids is one of the responsibilities, and it can work. When you're just running out to the store, it's reasonable to expect an older child to keep an eye on the younger kids. For longer stints you may want to negotiate with your oldest how much sitting is reasonable.

Amy's parents sat down with all three kids and worked out the rules and expectations for when Amy was babysitting. Then they talked to Amy about how to enforce the rules and role-played some of the more difficult situations. Bedtime was the real challenge. First, her parents reminded her that this was a challenge for them too, as the boys really didn't like going to bed. They suggested that she ask the boys to get ready for bed and a story, and then she should leave them to it rather than nag. It was the boys' responsibility to get themselves ready and into bed. And they added that if the younger boys were still up when the parents returned, they'd have to face the consequences.

Money is another sticky issue for families. It's reasonable to expect kids to look after their younger siblings. In many families, the parents will pay an older child if he has to turn down a paid job to stay home. You can choose how to handle this problem, but it's important that you address it and that everyone is clear on the expectations. When siblings are fewer than two years apart in age, it's generally best to have them share the responsibility, so they're home together without one necessarily being in charge. It's important to recognize the help the older child is offering and respect her schedule; so if she has a soccer game, for example, don't interfere with it.

Babysitting Guide for Parents

- Clarify the rules and expectations with all the children.
- Respect your teen's schedule.
- Recognize the help she's giving you in taking care of a younger sibling.
- If she turns down a paid job to stay with her siblings, pay her for the job.
- When the age difference is slight, don't set up the older to be in charge. Have them cooperate to be home without you.

IN OTHER WORDS ...

- If you have more than one child, some squabbling is to be expected.
- The primary reason for kids' squabbles is to get your attention.
- In learning how to handle their differences, kids are developing useful lifelong negotiating and problem-solving skills.
- Joint projects among siblings can help them develop team-building abilities.
- Having an older child babysit is acceptable and worthwhile, within limits.

TALKING ABOUT BEHAVIOR
Kathy's Q & A

QUESTION

I have a four-year-old boy and six-year-old girl who bicker constantly. It's driving me nuts. "She got more cereal than me." "He took the special spoon." They argue over every little thing. What can I do to help them get along better?

ANSWER

Siblings arguing, bickering and quarrelling is the complaint of almost every parent with more than one child. Those with only children complain that their kids bicker with friends as well as with them. They do it because it works. There's nothing as compeling as that high-pitched yell, "Mom, he won't let me ..." to make you come running to fix the problem. Children want our attention, and they learn early that fighting is the quickest and surest way to get us involved. We may try to reason, we may join the fray by taking sides, we may act as judge and jury as we try to determine who did what to whom and who did it first. Whatever our reaction, it's attention and it's often quite entertaining for the kids.

The solution is to refuse to participate. We need to wean them off our automatic presence. So although we appear, we do so in a calm and uninvolved manner. If they're fighting over a toy, we can simply remove it and in a quiet voice say that they can have it back when they figure out a solution. Meanwhile, if they want to join you folding laundry you could use the help. Later, when everything is calmer, you can help negotiate solutions to ongoing conflict areas. Let them come to solutions. If they're truly stuck, you can offer some suggestions: "How would it work if you took turns?" The more involvement they have, the more likely they are to follow through with the plan. When they bicker about a "non-problem," like who got more cereal, simply shrug. If you refuse to engage in the discussion, it will die. So a simple "Is that right?" followed by "Oh well, that's life" defuses a potential ongoing argument.

QUESTION

After a lovely summer with my two children ages eight and eleven, I dread the return of school and fights over homework. They're expected to get right to work when they get home from school, but they never do and the fight to get homework done lasts all evening. What can I do?

ANSWER

September is a perfect time to tackle this problem. It's the start of a new school year and can be the start of a new approach to homework for your children. First, meet with their teachers to find out just how much homework they'll have. This will not only give you the information you need but also demonstrate to the teacher and the kids that you plan on being involved. Then sit down with your children to develop a homework plan. Let them talk about their needs and wishes. When do they want to do homework? School is the work of children, and most want a break after their classes. Just as an adult who comes home from work with a bulging briefcase usually wants to rest and eat before he gets back to work, children generally need a snack and time to play before they tackle homework.

Where do they want to do homework? Lots of kids need a separate space like a desk in their bedroom, but some work best at the dining room table with the evening activity going on around them. You can support their plan by taking phone messages for them while they study and being available in case they need help. An encyclopedia and atlas are worthwhile investments if at all possible so that children can do research at home. Trips to the library are also important because they learn how to do research as well as borrowing books that match their interests, hobbies or dreams. If they're involved in setting the rules they're more likely to follow them. But remember, it's *their* homework, not yours. So once you've helped them develop a plan, let them take the responsibility.

QUESTION

Our five-year-old son and two-year-old daughter share the same room because we have only two bedrooms. Our son is perfectly happy with the arrangement and even says he doesn't want to be in a room by himself. At what age does it become inappropriate for siblings of opposite sex to share a room?

ANSWER

They'll let you know when the arrangement is no longer working for them. Many brothers and sisters with separate bedrooms in fact wind up together in one room because they're lonely, cold or frightened. As long as the arrangement works for them, don't worry about it. Generally, as children approach eight to ten years old, they start to want more privacy. When you notice your son locking the bathroom door or wanting no one to look when he's changing his clothes, it's time for separation. There may be a problem once he starts bringing friends home from school. It may be difficult for him to entertain when his little sister is right there. While you can insist on good manners all round, your son will need some space for entertaining away from his sister. Either identify another part of the house for this play or have the younger child help you around the house when her brother has friends in their room. Big houses with many separate spaces are fairly new. Our parents and grandparents often lived in close quarters and survived quite nicely.

CHAPTER 5

BUT WHY CAN'T I GET HIM TO TAKE OUT THE GARBAGE?

It happens often. I'm speaking to a group of parents of young teens when one parent says to me, "She's fourteen years old and won't even start supper for me. What can I do?" My response is a question: "When did you start teaching her how to cook? And when did you start expecting her to help with meal preparation?" All too often this is greeted with a blank stare and a repetition that after all she's fourteen years old and should be able to start dinner. But it's not inherent. While a youngster will reach puberty no matter what we do, she won't suddenly have the skills we think should follow. I'm fifty-nine-years-old and can't run wire to an electrical box. But I know lots of people, men and women, who can handle this task. At some point, they were taught. They did it with supervision, and now it's a skill they have. This is how we develop skills.

WHO NEEDS KIDS TODAY?

Kids today are unmotivated, take everything for granted, are lazy and have no respect for other people's property. Or so I'm told. And it's the fault of society, of television, of the school or even the grandparents. But playing the blame game isn't helpful. There are reasons why kids behave the way they do, and it makes more sense to figure out what's going on and deal with it rather than point fingers.

You're going away for a week. It could be business, it could be pleasure but, whatever it is, you'll be leaving the children at home. Well, trying to make all the arrangements for your children before you go can be daunting. Childcare, meals, scheduling for extracurricular events—it goes on and on. By the time you get to the airport you're exhausted from all the planning. Now, imagine your child is going away for a week. How many arrangements does he have to make before he leaves? I bet he can just pack and go. It's not fair. On the other hand, all the arrangements you need to make send you a message about your value. You need to cover all your responsibilities, all the things you'd normally take care of before you can leave. It's clear evidence that you have a role in this family and that you're needed.

Your child, on the other hand, gets no such message. He can stay or he can go—it really doesn't matter. Okay, okay, it matters to you. You'll miss him. But is his absence going to create more work for you? When you stop laughing, think about the implications. You're secure in the knowledge of your place, your importance in the family. He knows that you love him but that on a concrete level you don't really need him. Historically, children were needed. Historically, children were an economic asset to the family and society. Face it, if economics had been your only motivation, would you have had children? Do you *need* children? Are they essential to the running of your family or life? Of course not. But how did this situation develop?

After the Second World War, society decided to improve things for kids. The war was over; women returned home to full-time house and child care, and childhood was to be a carefree time. Children were going to enjoy childhood and have everything their parents (having lived through the Depression and war) never had. With this attitude came the belief that children shouldn't have to work. Children should just play. Childhood was carefree. As children played and didn't actively and concretely contribute, they started to be viewed as useless—cute, lovable, wanted and loved, but useless.

Today, our motivation has changed. We're all so busy, and having kids help just isn't efficient. Their inexpert "help" slows us down. If you were in a hurry, why would you ask a toddler to put on his own shoes or a preschooler to dress herself? You can do it in a minute and get on with the day; they'll take forever. But this is at the heart of some of the problems we're seeing today. Children know they're wanted and loved, but they also know they're not needed.

ADULT/CHILD TIME

Since the Second World War we've also moved from an essentially rural to an urban economy. Folks have moved in droves from the farms to the cities. Farming was a home-based business that required the help of all family members. And they often worked together. Paid work is done in an office, factory, store or on the road; children's work is done in school. Housework is often done while children are away at school, daycare, or preschool—and sometimes by people who aren't family members. Not only do children not participate with adults in work, but they don't observe it.

Children also have little understanding about the economics of work and family bills because banking is electronic. What's the problem? Just go to the machine and get some more money. It's going to be interesting over the next ten or twenty years to see how the growth of home-based businesses changes the way parents spend time with their kids. Their children may start to have some idea of what it is that mommy and daddy do for a living. But, even with that development, today's work doesn't often lend itself to multi-generational activities.

So how do we involve the kids? First, understand that our children love to work with us. When my son Foley was just three years old I watched him help his dad, John, put up drywall. John put a can of nails on a small, sturdy stool. He asked Foley to please get him a nail. Foley reached into the can, brought the nail to his father and watch as he hammered it into the stud. And the job was over. Now, he had a choice; he could stay and continue working with his dad or go and play. He chose to stay, and for two hours he diligently brought nails, one at a time, to his father. Was this the most efficient way for John to complete this job? Of course not. Usually he'd have the nails handy in his apron pocket and hammer away. But efficiency shouldn't always be the goal. The drywall made it onto the studs, our son learned about nails, drywall, and creating a solid wall, and the two had a great afternoon together. For years afterwards both could look at the wall and know they had built it together.

CHORES

Not all the jobs we do with our children are as interesting and dramatic as building a wall. We also need to involve them in the daily grind: doing the dishes, taking out the garbage, cleaning the toilet and dusting the coffee table. Somehow, we all know that kids should be helping out around the house, but it's such a hassle. It takes time, it takes patience, it takes training, and it takes supervision. What's the point when we can do it quickly ourselves and get on with our busy lives?

Why Work?

Children who are included in family work benefit by:

- feeling useful
- feeling necessary
- feeling competent
- being trusted

They learn:

- self-discipline
- promptness
- neatness
- reliability
- responsibility

Doing household chores is on-the-job training for independent living.

Children who have chores not only learn how to do the work, and that it does take work to run a household, they also know they're needed. Jennifer and Derek are two-year-old twins. One day a neighbor spotted them and their mom walking up to their house. Each child was carefully carrying a potato. Mom had a full shopping bag. They had just returned from a store that's five blocks away. When asked, the kids explained that Mom couldn't carry all the groceries and needed help, so she asked them to carry a potato each so that there'd be enough for supper that night. They handled those potatoes as if they were eggs. Once they got home, they eagerly told their dad what they had done. After supper, Dad thanked the kids for bringing home the potatoes that he'd so enjoyed for dinner that evening. Now, these kids know they're needed. And their mother knew just how to choose an appropriate task for them to handle. There was no downside. So what if one of them dropped the potato?

At the beginning of this chapter, I mentioned parents who expect that at a certain age, usually in the early teens, their children will suddenly become helpful around the house. The irony is that our toddlers and preschoolers love to help, and in the interests of time and efficiency, we put them off. But that's the perfect time to start. If we start involving them at a young age when they're keen, by the time they learn that they're not supposed to want to do housework it's too late; they're part of the family working group. The trick isn't just to permit our little ones to help, but to expect it. They need to learn that the work gets done whether we're in the mood or not. There's nothing wrong with making a job as enjoyable as possible, but I don't believe they always have to like it. I've never danced a jig of joy on my way to clean the toilet, but I did the job. So when they turn up their noses at the work, let them know that they don't have to like it, they just have to do it.

We also want to choose tasks that are developmentally appropriate. Carrying potatoes home from the store is a great job for a toddler. As kids get older we can entrust them with increasingly challenging chores. (And do make sure to teach both your boys and girls. In this day and age, boys need to know how to cook and clean and girls to change light bulbs and run the lawn mower.) With little ones it's also important that the job be completed in a very short time. So when your toddler is helping set the table, you can ask her to put the forks on the table. Then the job is finished. Your preschooler can set the table, although she may not get all the silverware in the right order. An older child sets the table and brings in the food that he helped prepare. In all cases, you note the contribution of the child and thank her.

It's not just about doing the work, it's about being involved in the process and knowing that without their help this meal wouldn't be on the table.

Some Chores Children Can Handle

Two-year-old

- stir dry ingredients when baking
- pick up toys with your help
- choose between two foods
- finish a zipper after it's started

Three-year-old

- set table
- dress self
- help make bed
- vacuum (on most models you can shorten the wand to kid-sized)

Four-year-old

- put groceries away on a low shelf
- feed pets
- dust
- answer phone

Five-year-old

- make simple sandwich
- pour drink
- walk short distances alone
- tie shoes

Six-year-old

- water plants and flowers
- straighten silverware drawer
- put away his laundry
- get self dressed for school

Seven-year-old

- run errands for parent
- care for bicycle
- get self up in morning
- fold laundry

Eight- to Nine-year-old

- mop floors
- sew buttons
- run own bath
- begin to read and follow simple recipes

Ten- to Eleven-year-old

- pack suitcase for trips
- handle self appropriately in public places with peers
- be responsible for homework
- cook a simple meal

CHORES AND CHILDREN

Okay, so I've convinced you. It's a good idea to involve kids in the running of the house and have them participate in the house-work. But how can we really make this happen without going crazy? Parents often tell me that the reason they don't involve kids in chores is that the traditional jobs for kids (like collecting eggs on the farm) just don't exist today. The list we've put together simply contains a few examples; take a look and you'll discover that there are lots of ways that kids can participate.

Another common complaint is that they just don't get to it. With younger kids, the solution is to work with them. If you watch your kids at daycare or preschool, you'll see that they happily and industriously work to do the pickup. Drives you nuts, doesn't it; why don't they do it at home? The reason is that at preschool they're part of a team, working together to make it happen. So, try that at home. Work together. With older kids it's still neat to work with them as much as possible, but they can be expected to handle a task like vacuuming the living room on their own. Be sure, though, to involve them in the decision and to set a deadline by which it must be done.

Consulting with kids on chores and planning is always a good idea. In my previous book, *Who's In Charge Anyway?*, there's a full chapter on family meetings, which is the best place for determin-ing chores. When kids get to choose their chores they're more committed to getting the work done. One method is to simply create a list of chores for the week and let each family member choose in turn until the list is finished. Mind you, that only works when the children are close in age. When there's an age spread, the choices can be offered by age so that the older kids take on the more challenging work. Besides feeling some ownership for a chosen chore because she got to choose it, having choices eliminates boredom. Some kids don't resent helping out: they resent having to take out the garbage week after week, year after year. But ask them to wash the kitchen floor or clean the bathroom and you have compliance.

Let's face it: one drawback to having kids do housework is that they just don't do it well enough. For picky housekeepers (and this doesn't include me!) no one will ever do it well enough; but that's another issue. You do need to set the standards to meet the age. A preschooler who vacuums will only do the middle of the room. The corners will happily continue to produce dust balls. And you need to live with that. But this is the advantage of having them choose chores. You can make sure that you get to vacuum next time and do all the spots they missed. But if you follow them around and re-do all their work, they'll never work cheerfully for you. On the other hand, a ten-year-old who vacuums only the middle of the room can be called back. A great line to use in this situation is, "You made a good start, now how about you finish the job?"

You also need to ask yourself if you taught your child how to do the job. We tend to think that most of the chores we assign our kids are so simple and obvious that they should just know what to do. Well, trust me, they don't. Just because they've been living with you all of their lives and watching you do the work doesn't mean they know what's expected or how to do it. It's like when you first start to drive. You've been a passenger all your life and now you're ready to head off to the mall and you suddenly aren't sure of the route. I followed the bus trolley wires for the first days as a driver because I knew the bus routes. I had to pay attention on the bus to know when to get off. So show your kids how to do the job. Go through the steps with them and teach them how to do the work. And, of course, you're the model. Your standards of cleanliness and neatness, along with your attitude to housework, will be a strong factor in how they view and do the work.

IN OTHER WORDS ...

- Kids today know they're wanted and loved but not that they're needed.
- It's our job to help them know that they're needed in the family, and one sure way to accomplish this is to have them help with the housework.
- Work around the house teaches valuable life skills and give kids a sense of competence.

TALKING ABOUT BEHAVIOR
Kathy's Q & A

QUESTION

My four-year-old won't pick up her toys. She knows the rule, but every time I send her to the playroom to put away her things, she just plays some more until I show up and start hollering. Help!

ANSWER

The answer lies in your question. You say that when you show up she starts picking up her toys. What you now want to do is examine what you're doing besides hollering. Are you giving her direction? Parents often can't understand their children's inability to handle as simple a chore as picking up after themselves. (Mind you, adults often complain that their spouses and roommates leave their stuff lying around.) For preschoolers, the task of picking up can be overwhelming. Often they don't do the job because they just can't figure out where to start, so they just do nothing and keep playing.

Our first task is to teach these children. We forget that tasks that seem simple to us can be new and confusing for them. So, give direction. "The blocks go in this box, so why don't you put them away first." Preschoolers are rarely self-disciplined enough to work alone. They love to work with us. So make toy pickup a joint task, and you and your child will find that the job will go quickly and pleasantly. Toy pickup becomes easier when there are lots of containers for the toys with many pieces. I also recommend shelves rather than toy boxes for storage. It's difficult for children to choose toys from a toy box, so they tend to empty the whole thing. Shelves allow children to see and choose the toy they want, so they're less likely to dump toys all over the floor.

QUESTION

My seven-year-old will always find something or someone else to take the blame for his actions, even when it's obvious he's at fault. How can I get him to accept the consequences of his actions?

ANSWER

Taking the consequences for your mistakes or negative actions isn't easy for anyone, particularly children. When you know that he's at fault in a situation, it's best to move onto the consequences without engaging him in the argument about who or what's at fault. If your attitude is, "This happened and now it needs to be dealt with," it's harder for him to argue. For example, if you find toys strewn all around the living room, talk about the mess. Don't deal with how they got there. "There are toys all over the floor, do you want to pick up the Lego first or the balls?" When he starts to blame someone else, simply repeat yourself. "The point is, these toys must be picked up. Do you want to pick up the Lego first, or the balls?" When he takes responsibility for the pickup, he's dealing with the consequences without having to accept the blame.

You can also connect the consequence to his own choice when he breaks a clear rule. Instead of demanding, "Did you break this rule?" you can simply say, "By breaking the rule you've chosen to handle the consequences." Note that I say "consequence," not "punishment." There's a clear difference between discipline and punishment. With punishment, the goal is to cause pain or discomfort so that the child will want to avoid the behavior in future. He doesn't want to be hurt again. With discipline, our goal is to teach our children about the rules and the ramifications of breaking them. The description above is an example of discipline because you're teaching him how to deal with making the mess. By saying he can't play video games for a week, you might get his attention, but that would be punishment. Kids who are punished are more likely to try to avoid the blame in order to avoid the pain or discomfort. When they're disciplined they can deal with their wrong choices and then get on with their lives. It's all about attitude.

QUESTION

My ten-year-old is pestering us for a raise in her allowance. She now gets four dollars a week and uses most of it to buy treats. I don't want her tanking up on candy and pop, but I do want to be fair. I've talked to other parents, and it seems the amount of allowance they give is all over the map, from nothing to more than ten dollars a week. What's appropriate for kids of this age?

ANSWER

The purpose of an allowance isn't just to buy treats. It's to help children learn about money management. As you've discovered, there's no magic number for an allowance by age. You may want to sit down with her and develop a plan. What should she be expected to buy from her allowance? Does she buy lunch at school? Pay to rent movies or video games? She may be expected to save to buy Christmas gifts or extra toys or clothing. Candy and other treats are also typically included in this list. Once you've determined her needs, you can then determine the amount of money. Asking her to pay for more than just junk food will help her to set priorities. For example, if she spends all her money on treats, she won't have any left to go with you to see the latest movie. It's a good idea for ten-year-olds to get their allowance weekly because they find it difficult to budget over a longer period. There's a book out by Paul Lermitte that will interest you called *Allowances, Dollars and Sense*.

CHAPTER 6

SHE CAN DO IT HERSELF

It was a Tuesday in March. I was at the Vancouver Aquarium gift shop buying souvenirs. I made my purchases and wandered outside, where there are a number of pools and exhibits. The building is all glass on that side, so you can see right into it. It was a quiet day; there was myself, a young mom pushing a stroller with a baby and a father with his four-year-old daughter. Dad was taking advantage of being outdoors to have a cigarette. The four-year-old announced that she was getting cold and wanted to go inside. Dad suggested she go ahead, and he'd meet her in a minute. She could either just wait inside the glass doors or head down the hall to the shark tank. She didn't demure or complain. She became instantly hysterical. She was screaming and crying as she said, "You can't send me in there! I'll be stolen!" Her bemused father tried to reason with her: he'd be able to see her the whole time, it was a safe place; but there was no consoling her. She was terrified.

What are we doing to our children? There are so many stories of children who are afraid of everyone and everything. There are even more stories of parents who won't let their children out of their sight. One mom proudly told me that she takes her grade four child all the way to his classroom door and doesn't leave until she sees the teacher. Another announced that her eleven-year-old has never been out of sight of either herself, her dad or a caregiver. Children are being handed off like precious cargo from one adult to another. How will our kids ever look after themselves if they never get the chance to learn?

MISSING KIDS

Why are we hovering over our children? What are we afraid of? Ask almost any parent, and they'll tell you that it's a dangerous world out there. The scariest thought of all is that your child just might be abducted. And that's frightening. But is our fear in proportion to reality? The odds of any child, of *your* child, being snatched are infinitesimal. Most missing children are habitual runaways. While the numbers look staggering, seventy-five percent are kids reported missing multiple times. In fact, there can be as many as twenty reports on one child. In other words, the number of reported cases of missing kids doesn't represent that many different individuals. Of those who are actually abducted, family members grab the majority, usually as part of a custody dispute. However, if your child goes missing, you simply don't care about statistics. If you sent your child out to play and he didn't come home, you'd never forgive yourself. Boy, we all understand that! But is our fear reasonable? Are we really helping our kids?

Let's take a look. In most cases we choose to drive our children places to ensure that they're supervised at all times. But, according to the Children's Hospitals in Toronto and Vancouver, the most common cause of childhood injury and death is automobile accidents. Somehow we feel that we have some control with our children in the car and that we lose that control if we let them out on their own. But our feelings don't match the facts. If we went with the raw data, we'd never let them in the car. We're being good parents. We care about our kids. Ask anyone who does let their children walk to school or go ahead of them into the Aquarium and they'll tell you that they don't get the support of other parents. They're sometimes seen as not doing their job.

While we're busy protecting our children, what are they learning? The little girl at the Aquarium has learned to be terrified. Children are learning that we don't trust them to handle situations on their own. And they don't learn the skills they'll need when they finally step out on their own.

SAFETY IS AS SAFETY DOES

I was curled up warm and comfy during a recent and extremely rare snowstorm in Vancouver, watching the news on TV. The story was that elementary schools were still open after a snowfall of five to ten centimeters. In Vancouver, any snow is big news. The TV reporter was poking a mike in the window of a car, and the mom at the wheel was explaining that she was unhappy the schools were open because she wasn't comfortable driving her child to school in the snow.

I started to think about other stories we've read in the papers lately. There are the stories about childhood obesity. Our kids are getting fatter, and more of them are suffering, or will suffer, physical ailments as a result. I read that children, even very young kids, are becoming increasingly sedentary, which goes against nature, I would think. Which brings me back to the snowstorm. Why is a mom, uncomfortable driving in snow, in her car? Most parents who drive their kids to school do so to keep the kids safe. But how can it be safer for kids to ride in a car driven by a nervous and unskilled (in the snow) driver? Safer than what? Imagine if these same kids and all the kids in the neighborhood walked, ran, skipped and jumped their way home. Then they could build a snowman, have a snowball fight and make angels on their newly white lawns.

Kids who live within walking distance of their school should get themselves to school. They need the exercise. They need the social time with their friends. And they need the transition from home to school, time to think of themselves not as "mommy's little angel" but as "Mr. Porter's student." They need to see themselves as someone capable of getting from point A to point B.

So what do you do if you live too far away or the kids have to cross an unprotected and busy intersection? Think of the goals. We want our children to get the exercise, to have the social time, to make the transition and to move toward independence. One mom I know, whose children had to cross a very busy street, walked her kids across and then left them to finish the trip on their own. The safety needs were handled, and all other goals met. We need to be clear on the goals and figure out how, in our particular situation, we can accomplish them. But there's pressure on parents—

pressure to physically supervise our children each and every hour of each and every day. It just doesn't feel safe out there. That's why we prepare them. We make sure they know the way to and from school; we ensure that they're not walking alone. If we all open our doors in the morning and send our kids on their way, there will be lots of kids on the sidewalks, all going in the same direction. It's our job to give our children the tools they need and their job to use those tools.

THE PARENTS' ROLE IN SCHOOL

Sarah's son, Braden, is a grade eleven student in the local high school. Sarah has always been involved in the school parent committee. One day she was at the school in the afternoon. She'd told her son that if he wanted to meet her after her meeting, they could go home together. Braden found her walking down the hall with the principal; both were laughing and joking, and clearly enjoying each other's company. On the way home Braden mentioned that he didn't think of his principal as a guy who even smiled, let alone laughed. You see, it's a huge school, and the students deal with the vice principals and see the principal only occasionally, at very formal occasions. Seeing this glimpse of his principal in another role changed Braden's thinking about the school's administration.

Even though volunteering at the school can seem to some like a waste of time, it's important. Studies have shown that kids who see their parents involved in their school get a clear message that school matters, and they tend to do better. Involved parents get to know their way around, meet the teachers, counselors and administrators informally and feel comfortable in the building. As a result, if their child does have a problem, the parent can approach not only the right person but also someone with whom they already have a relationship. The trick is to be clear on the roles. Most parent committees have guidelines outlining the function of the members, and there are other ways to be involved as well. I want to underline that if it's at all possible, parents need to make the effort.

However you choose to support your school, it's important to be clear on the roles of student, teacher and parent in your child's education. Generally, the teacher teaches, your child is responsible for schoolwork and the parent plays a support role. However, you do enter the picture as an advocate when the situation is beyond the ability of your child. For example, bullying requires both parents and teachers to get involved. Or if you have a child with special needs, he'll need you as an advocate.

HOMEWORK

Whether or not you volunteer at the school, homework will enter your life. Most parents dread homework more than their off-spring. What is your role? Well, the most important thing to remember is that this is your child's homework. You did yours. Now it's his turn. Not having to do homework is one of the perks of being the parent. Your job is to be supportive. Make sure he has a place to work. Develop with him a time when he'll work, and be available as a consultant if necessary.

A consultant drives her child to the library if he needs to do research, or shows the child how to use the family's encyclopedia or conduct an online search. She then leaves the child to do the work. As a consultant you need to avoid looking up the material for the child, printing it out or highlighting the relevant para-graphs. You teach him how to do it and then let him get on with it. If he chooses to daydream rather than work, that's his problem, and then he'll have to deal with his teacher.

In terms of where or when he does his homework there's no hard and fast rule. Homework may have to be scheduled around extracurricular activities. There are some who believe that it should be done right after school, but that only works for some children. Not all kids are ready to settle down to schoolwork until they've had a break, a snack and some playtime. Some kids need a nice quiet environment, but others do much better right in the middle of things at the kitchen table. If you think of some open-plan workplaces, this doesn't seem so weird.

SUMMER CAMP

Summer camp, or any travel to places without parents, is another golden opportunity for our children to develop independence. Camp is great because it's designed to meet the developmental needs of your children, with challenges and opportunities appropriate to their age. I can still see my children heading off to camp. In each case, a nervous and excited little kid would board the bus or boat. As it pulled away, they'd be frantically waving at us, suddenly not sure if they were ready for this step. I never cried until they were out of sight. Then we'd have to figure out how to spend the next two weeks with only the odd letter. And some of those letters from camp are truly odd.

Two weeks later, Chelsea or Foley would return, and we'd be waiting anxiously. We wanted to scoop them up immediately, but they'd wave us off. They had to say goodbye; they had to collect their stuff. They were almost back with us, but not quite. Each time they went to camp they came home with increased self-confidence and a sense of triumph, having grown a little more as independent people. They had made it without us and (since they'd been at different camps) without each other. And they'd had fun doing it. They could choose to tell us about it, or not. Now I read in the paper that there's a movement to wire summer camps—to put cameras around the campsite so mom and dad can take a look and see what's happening. There are children who email home daily. Boy, are they missing the point!

CHOICES

Our long-term goal is to raise independent children. And that means knowing how to make responsible choices. Letting our children make choices can be extremely difficult. But it's the only way they'll learn to look before they leap, to think about what they're about to do and consider the possible outcomes. It takes experience to make mature decisions, and the sooner we start letting them gather this experience, the easier it will be for all of us. Some decisions are easy. Well, easy for us, at any rate. Letting Susie decide what to wear when she goes to play with her friend doesn't cause our blood pressure to rise at all. Depending on her personality and age, it may be agonizing for her, but even if she asks, resist the temptation to intervene. Let her decide and live with her decision. Even if it turns out it wasn't the right choice, she'll learn but not die. It's safe and simple for us to let our kids choose what to wear, how to style their hair or their extracurricular activities. Even when they're little we can start letting them make choices: red pajamas or blue? Sweater or jacket? Apple or orange? Each choice with its subsequent consequences creates the experience bank they'll need when the choices become more serious.

Some other choices are more difficult. Penny has been taking piano lessons for five years and suddenly wants to stop. Should she be permitted to make this choice? I'd say yes. She can always return to piano at another time in her life. Meanwhile, do you really want to fight with her every night to make her practice? She may simply need a break, or she may want to try something new, but whatever the situation, she's the one who has to want to play piano.

Choices can get harder. What about kids who don't want to visit Grandma? Or kids who no longer want to go to church? Well, what are your family values on this topic? There's no right answer. It simply comes down to, "Is it worth the fight?" and it may well be. In our house, if it had to do with family, the kids were expected to participate as family members. Sometimes, however, there are compromises that have to be made. The kids can join you for dinner but can then politely excuse themselves. Perhaps they don't have to go to church every week. This is your choice. See, I told you making choices could be difficult.

What about when they're about to blow it? So here they are, learning about choices and their consequences. All of which implies that they'll sometimes make the wrong choice. And most often you can see it coming. What's your role? It depends on the age of the child and the seriousness of the choice. We're still the parents and while we want our kids to learn, we don't want them to be devastated. Your eight-year-old insists on buying the toy advertised on the back of the cereal box. You tell him you have seen these sorts of toys before, and they're usually junk. He's adamant. Assuming he has saved enough money, let him buy it, and if (when) it breaks don't lecture. Be sympathetic, and let him learn the lesson.

Seventeen-year-old Jasmine became extremely involved in volunteer work at the local senior's center. Some of her friends worked with her so it was a time for socializing as well as for being generous. Her parents were thrilled but also concerned about the amount of time she spent at the center. She assured them that she had it all in order. But her first report card told a different story. Her marks meant that she'd graduate, but post-secondary education would be out of reach. So her parents asked her if she was planning on university. The answer was yes. "Therefore," her father told her, "you can only go to the center one evening a week." Jasmine's parents had let her try to balance school and volunteer work, and she failed. Now, in view of her wish to go to university, she'd have to spend a lot more time on her studies. Her parents couldn't let her compromise her marks without intervening. Mind you, doing the studying was still her responsibility.

ISOLATION

Human beings are social animals. Children who are connected to many adults receive the accumulated wisdom of the people in their circle. Over-protection denies our kids this resource. We've become so nervous about our children's safety that we've nar-rowed down their potential relationships. Not only have we taught our children to avoid and be wary of any person they don't know, we're asking the adults we do bring into their lives to be our clones.

In my open-line radio appearances I often hear from parents concerned that the children's relatives, grandparents and aunts and uncles, don't share all their parenting values. Are they bad people? Are they doing anything to hurt the children? No, they just think differently. My response is that this is a gift. Children need to meet and form relationships with all kinds of folks if they're to learn about the world. Uncle Harvey may smoke a stinky cigar and sometimes use salty language but, boy, can he tell your kids great fishing stories.

Smaller families often mean that kids live with only one or no siblings and one or two parents. They go to school with kids their own age, and all their programs are for kids their age. It's a pretty small lens through which to study the world about them. Then, because we're worried about their safety, we ask them to come straight home from school, double lock all the doors and wait for us to come home.

But kids are social animals by nature. So they go online. We worry about how much time they spend with their anonymous and invisible cyber-buddies. So we teach them to be careful, not to give out personal information when using the computer. That's a good thing. But it's better to permit and encourage face-to-face time. Let them play with their friends. Have a neighborhood meeting; invite all the kids. The parents can set parameters and expectations for the whole group of kids. Now all the adults know all the kids, the rules are universal, and your kids are associating with real live people. And as a bonus, they're meeting all the different adults up and down the block. Of course, this won't work in all neighborhoods. Maybe only one family is interested in getting together; if so, that's still a good place to start.

QUASI ADULTS

Another challenge of the new millennium is the perceived speed with which kids are growing up. Look at them. No longer do we see grubby little kids playing in the dirt. They're in designer clothing. They shop at Baby Gap. I've heard of little girls having spa treatments for their ninth birthday party. Now it's one thing for kids to fool around playing dress-up, but it's another when the clothing and makeup are seen as regular clothing, not as play. I also read about a chance for girls (yes, it does seem to focus on girls) to have a tea party in a high-end restaurant, complete with all the trimmings. Again, the problem is that this isn't seen as play, as little girls pretending to be grown-up while knowing it's just a game.

It's more difficult for children to develop true independence when adult expectations are foisted on them as pre-teens. Independence is a process. Our eight-year-old daughters may have access to more information, more choices and more wardrobe than ever before. But although they look like teenagers, they're still little girls, with the decision-making skills that fit a pre-teen. It's an interesting dichotomy. We see many children who are over-protected and over-supervised, but they dress like kids many years older. How confusing is that? The challenge is to permit our kids to do for themselves what they can, when they're ready. We don't want them to be asked to act or be older than their developmental readiness, but at the same time we don't want to hold them back because we're afraid to let go. It's not easy, but then parenting, like all rewarding jobs, isn't always easy.

MICRO-MANAGING

Mary is busy on the phone. It's obvious that she's doing a selling job and equally clear that she's not going to hang up until she gets what she wants. Is she a super salesman promoting a product line? Well no, she's a mom working to get Cassandra on the elite soccer team. Cassandra is ten years old and slated to play on the community team, but according to Mary this just isn't good enough. Mary wants to have her play in the adjoining municipality where she'll have a better chance at making the regional finals.

It's a complex world we live in today, and managing the scheduling of our children's extracurricular activities can be daunting at best. But for many parents, that's just the start. They want a guarantee that their child will be on the best team, be in the top group and have the most enriching experience. Sounds good, like something parents should aspire to. Well, yes and no. Kids need to be a part of their community, and unless she's an elite performer in sports or the arts (which brings us down to a tiny percentage of all children), Cassandra can excel in her neighborhood with her friends. Every time we take over to change the rules for our children, we give them a message that they don't have to play by the rules or deal with the world they're handed. We give them the message that they're somehow too good for the mainstream. If Cassandra is, in fact, an elite level player she'll shine wherever she plays. Otherwise, as a good and keen player she should be playing within the rules of her community.

BUT WE CAN'T JUST LET THEM GO

In my first book, *Who's In Charge Anyway?* I told you that you're responsible for raising your children. And that's true. However, a big part of raising our kids is teaching them to be independent. The trip from total dependence to independence starts with the first breath your newborn takes and leads to the day she leaves home to live on her own. Our job is to support and encourage, as well as to expect and demand, the growing independence of our children. Somehow we've created a belief that in order to do our job, we need to hover over our kids day and night. A good parent is always there. But if moving to independence is a process, it requires that when they're ready, we back off and let them grow up. It's a case of determining the line between over-protection and supervision.

IN OTHER WORDS ...

- It's our job to support, encourage and permit our children to become independent when they're ready.
- It's not as dangerous out there as we think, and we have to let our children live in the world.
- Making choices is an important step to becoming a capable adult.

TALKING ABOUT BEHAVIOR
Kathy's Q & A

QUESTION
Our seven-year-old is constantly losing his jacket, mitts, snow pants, hoods, you name it. We've tried talking to him about the importance of caring for his belongings. We've tried other consequences, like confiscating video games and restricting TV-watching, but nothing seems to work. We don't feel we can just send him to school without mittens, saying, "Too bad, you lost them." Please help.

ANSWER
In the busy life of a seven-year-old, keeping track of boring (to him) things like mittens just doesn't take priority. The trick is to help him to want to arrive home with all his clothing. Try to make it easier for him to remember. Attaching mittens to sleeves and having hoods that are part of his jacket will certainly help. Involve him in buying his clothing so that he's aware of the cost and process of selection, and so that he likes what he has. If he really thinks his mittens are cool, he's more likely to want to keep

track of them. Once he's helped with the purchase, he'll feel more ownership and hence responsibility. He does need to learn that there are consequences for losing his belongings. When the consequences are logically related to his behavior, it'll be easier for him to make the connection.

For example, when he comes home without his snow pants, take him back to look for them. The time that he spent looking is time he can't spend watching his favorite TV program. This isn't arbitrary; it's logical. Or you can have him pay part of the cost of replacement. He'll need to use part of his allowance to buy new snow pants. You can decide how much he should contribute to the purchase. Decide what you're going to do, and do it. Lecturing a seven-year-old simply doesn't work, but action does. It's tempting to start offering rewards in a situation like this, but then he's not being responsible for the right reasons. However, a celebration of achievement is always in order. If he does manage to hang onto his stuff for a week or a month or so, a trip to the ice cream store or his favorite pizza place is a great idea.

QUESTION

How can I best teach my child to become responsible and self-motivated in getting schoolwork and chores completed, rather than having me nag and remind her all the time?

ANSWER

Teaching our children to be responsible and self-motivated is a process. As they grow and develop, their ability to take responsibility for schoolwork, chores and their social life increases. Our job is to guide and direct them to this level of independence. It starts with training and consequences. It often seems that whatever we're asking of the kids is self-evident, and they should just know how to do it. For example, why do they persist in dropping their belongings on the floor? Can't they see the mess it makes? Well, actually,, they simply don't care. So they need to see some results. When they start to watch television you can say, "When you've put away your belongings you can watch TV." If their lunch box is there, you could just leave it and let them deal with it in the morning or at lunch the next day.

Planning is also key. Doing homework is a source of conflict in many homes. Sitting down with your child and planning with her where and when she'll do her homework is helpful. Let her make some choices. Would she prefer to do it before dinner or afterwards? When kids get to make choices, they're more likely to follow through. Then let her take on the responsibility. Trust that she'll handle it and if she doesn't, let her handle the consequences. Now comes the really hard part. Stop reminding and nagging. They say that whenever you meet a child who always forgets, she has a parent who always remembers. Once she knows that you're leaving it to her, she'll learn to follow through on her responsibilities.

QUESTION

My son is thirteen and starting to use his own money for entertainment (going to movies with friends and so on). He would like to get a debit card before the holidays so that he can take money out of his bank account when and where he chooses. I've explained to him the security issues, the fees involved and the need to control spending in the face of easy withdrawals. He's suggested that he maintain two bank accounts, one for long-term saving and one with a small quantity of cash for spending. I think that he's responsible enough, but my husband doesn't like the idea. Suggestions?

ANSWER

It sounds as if your son has thought through the issues and can be trusted to handle a debit card. In fact, it's probably safer for him to take out money as he needs it rather than carrying it in his wallet. The bank can adjust his ability to withdraw money. When he applies go with him and have them set a fairly low daily limit until you're confident that he can control his spending. Kids need to learn how to handle money, and debit cards are a definite part of how we access and spend money today. It's a good idea for teens to learn how to use these cards responsibly while they have a low spending limit and can't get themselves into too much trouble.

QUESTION

We just moved into a quiet cul-de-sac, and I've noticed the neighborhood kids seem to go from house to house by themselves (I'm talking about five-year-olds). My own five-year-old daughter would like to join in, but I'm reluctant to let her. Am I being overprotective?

ANSWER

When we were kids we played up and down the street all day. Today, the rules have changed. We're more nervous about our children's safety. This is partly because media coverage of outrages against children receives front page coverage even when it happened halfway around the world. It's also because we see more violence on television and in the movies, which make us hesitant to let our children out of our sight. Our parents were comfortable letting us loose in the neighborhood because they knew everyone and everyone knew them and us. Not only was I in and out of neighbors houses, so were my parents.

I think you should let your daughter join the other children. But first, get to know your neighbors. A cul-de-sac party is a great idea. Whether it's a coffee and dessert party at your home or a joint barbecue in your yard, you'll meet everyone.

Talk to the parents of the other children. They may also have had concerns when they first let their children go out alone.

Have your daughter let you know where she is when she's out. She can pop her head in when she moves from one place to another, or she can give you a call. It sounds like you have a great situation for children. Relax and let her join the other kids.

CHAPTER 7

WHEN LIFE THROWS KIDS A CURVE

It was mid-December and a group of parents were chatting as they waited to pick up their three-year-olds from preschool. They talked about how excited their kids were about the upcoming pre-school Christmas party. One mom commented that she hadn't told her son about the party because she didn't want to have to deal with his excitement and, more importantly, if something happened and he couldn't attend, she didn't want him to know that he had missed it. "What if he gets sick?" she asked.

Missing out on activities because of illness is a reality of life. It's one of the myriad curves that life can throw at us, and we need to allow our children to learn how to cope. It would be nice to think we can protect our children from all misfortune, but as we all know, this is impossible. When we allow them to handle their particular reality, with our support, right from a young age, they'll develop the necessary skills and become stronger.

DEATH AND GRIEVING

When Sally was four years old, her mother died. Despite her young age her dad brought her to the funeral with the rest of the family. Only a year later her father died, and the adults in charge decided she was too young to attend the funeral. Her older sister tried to get them to change their minds by pointing out that she had been included the previous year, but to no avail. Sally doesn't really remember either time, but she knows in her heart that she never got to say goodbye to her father. She's now fifty, and her non-attendance at her father's funeral still rankles. In trying to protect her, the adults denied her the culturally appropriate forms we have for handling grief. They assumed she wouldn't notice, and that grief is too big an emotion for such a young child. They had all the best intentions but made the wrong decision. The death of a loved one is tough. The death of a loved one who dies young is extremely tough. It's natural to want to protect our children from tough situations. The irony is that the protection often backfires, as it did with Sally. Had she been included in the rest of the family at the funeral, she'd have a much healthier feeling about it today, forty-five years later.

Children have different levels of understanding about death. Young children will respond to the people around them. They'll be concerned that the adults are unhappy and crying. They'll certainly notice that their schedules have changed and that many people are coming and going. When a parent dies, children aren't dealing only with all the issues that surround a death, they'll have lost the very person they could have turned to for support in this difficult time. And the remaining parent is also devastated. When my mother died, my father was suddenly left with four young, confused and grieving daughters. Somehow, he managed to put his needs aside and look after us. Many years later I learned that at night, after we were asleep, he'd go to the nearby home of his best friend to talk and unwind. He saved his needs until the end of the day. As a child, I simply accepted that he was there to care for me. As an adult, I have come to realize just how heroic his efforts were. It was an example of amazing parenting.

WHAT CHILDREN NEED

They need simple information. For most kids, what they imagine is more devastating than the truth. So, tell them what happened and use real language. If you say, "Grandma went to sleep and didn't wake up," she'll be afraid of sleep for you or herself. Say "Grandma died. She lived a long life, and it was time for it to end. She won't come back, but we can remember her." In the description make sure that your child understands that she played no role in what happened. Kids see the world through their own filters and often blame themselves when bad things happen. "If I had been a good girl," they think, "she wouldn't have died." So give them the facts: it was a car accident; she got sick; she was too old to live any longer. Facts will free them from bizarre and inaccurate thoughts. Then answer their questions when and if they come.

With preschoolers, you may have to explain what happened over and over again. They'll have lots of questions about the details of what happens to the body. They may also react to the death by becoming clingy or whiney so will need lots of reassurance. Six- to eight-year-olds know that death is irreversible. They'll have questions about the afterlife. And they'll ask the tough question, "Will you die too?" Just like the younger children, some kids feel responsible for the death. They may think that because they got mad at Grandpa, he died. So you need to explain what happened and make it clear that it was no one's fault. You also need to reassure them that the person who died is in no pain, that being buried or cremated doesn't hurt once you're dead. They may confuse the crying and think everyone is concerned that the dead person is hurting. So tell them that the tears are because you miss the person.

Nine- to fourteen-year-olds may experience intense feelings. They're at a stage when any emotions are often acute, and grief is no exception. Some children are worried that if they let themselves have the feeling, they won't be able to control it. If they start to cry, they'll never stop. Those children can appear unfeeling. We need to hold them and create an environment that allows them to express the feelings that are taking over their bodies. When Janice was twelve years old, her father died and she held herself back from the emotions that threatened to take over. Two weeks later she developed a nasty flu. Her family always wondered whether that was her body's way of handling the built-up emotion.

How Children Understand Death

- Toddlers respond to the emotions of those around them and notice the absence of the departed person.
- Preschoolers don't understand that death is permanent.
- School-age children need lots of details about death and dying.
- Tweens and young teens experience intense emotions, even if they hide them.
- Be prepared for morbid questions about what happens to the body. Young children are particularly concerned about all the details.

Helping Children Deal with Grief

- No matter how difficult it is, make sure you take the time to look after your children despite your grief.
- At the same time allow others to help you with child care.
- Be honest with your children about what happened and how badly you feel.
- Use straightforward language. Uncle Jim isn't sleeping; he's dead.
- Let them know that how they feel is okay.
- Allow them to participate in the rituals surrounding the death.
- If anyone in the family isn't coping, use the services of a professional grief counselor.

At some point we're all going to experience the death of a friend or family member. We don't do our children any favors when we try to protect them from the realities of life and death. If we include them in the family grieving and rituals, we let them know that they can handle this and that we'll both teach and support them. We teach them how to handle it by modeling, by answering their questions and by allowing them the space to experience their feelings of loss. Through the process they also learn that life does go on.

SUGAR MAKES ME SICK

When Allan was two years old he flew with his mother, Gloria, from Vancouver to Ottawa. It's a four-and-a-half hour flight with a three-hour time change. We picked them up at the airport and headed home. Allan had been playing happily in the other room when he suddenly walked in. His face was chalk white, with sweat beaded on his tiny brow. His eyes looked unfocussed. He came right up to me and said, "I need sugar." Gloria immediately told me that grape juice is the fastest sugar. I quickly poured him a glass. His color returned immediately, and I was asked to give him some protein. Cheese did the trick. Allan is diabetic. Because of the travel and time change that day, his blood sugar got out of whack, and he needed some sugar to stabilize his metabolism.

Kids with a medical condition challenge the whole family. And letting that child become independent can be the greatest challenge of all. Allan was diagnosed at fourteen months of age. Once he was stabilized and his family knew what he needed to stay healthy, they then needed to learn that only Allan was diabetic. That sounds reasonable and easy, but it's probably the most difficult task of all. It's hard to let any child go out into the world. How do we let him go when a simple mistake could cause a major medical problem?

Allan's parents started Allan on the path to independence as soon as he could talk. They didn't teach him to say "Mommy" or "Daddy," they taught him to say "Sugar makes me sick" and "I'm diabetic." They taught him what he could and couldn't eat. And, more importantly, they taught him to let them know when he had blown it. "Better," they said, "to know he couldn't resist the chocolate cake at the birthday party than to suddenly have this very ill child in the middle of the night, too ill to explain what happened." As soon as he was able, Allan learned to inject his insulin and, by his teens, he was testing his blood and determining his insulin and food needs. He's now a healthy, bright and capable young man in his early twenties.

WHY IS DADDY HOME ALL DAY?

The McMahon family had a well-established daily routine. In the morning, Mom got up first, followed quickly by Dad. Once they were finished in the bathroom it was time for six-year-old Sophie and eight-year-old Gabriella to start their day. Dad was first to leave in the morning, and then the girls headed off to school.

Mom worked in the afternoons so she saw them off on their way. The girls attended an after-school program every day, and Dad would pick them up. One day they noticed that when Dad picked them up, he wasn't his usual good-natured self. After dinner their parents huddled over the kitchen table talking in hushed voices. The next morning Dad didn't leave for work but wouldn't say why. The girls were confused and worried. Their world had changed, and they had no idea why. Finally, their parents sat them down and explained that Daddy had been laid off from work. It was almost a relief. The girls had imagined the worst, and feared that either Mom or Dad was sick and dying.

Parental unemployment can be devastating for children when they have no idea what's happening. Their life changes. Their parents look worried but won't talk to them about the problem, and their fears are often worse than reality. Children know something is going on, so talk to them. Tell them what has happened and reassure them that you'll handle it. If there's any immediate impact, like canceling a planned holiday or taking them out of daycare, let them know in a matter-of-fact manner. Older children may want or need to help, so recruit them and let them contribute to the family by helping care for the little ones or handing their babysitting money over to their parents. While you want to tell them the truth about what's happening, don't use them as a sounding board for your fears. They need to know that while there may be some changes, you'll look after them.

WHEN THE MARRIAGE FAILS

Hannah is the mother of four children. When she and her husband separated, the children ranged in age from four to twelve. Except for Daddy being out of the house, on the surface not much changed: Mom and the kids stayed in the family home, the children continued in the same school and daycare, and they still had their friends close by. Hannah was busy adjusting to her new life, going for counseling, joining support groups and figuring out how to make single friends. A year after the separation, Hannah and I were having coffee. I asked about her children and she said with some surprise in her voice, "You know, I think the separation actually had some effect on the kids." She told me that one of her kid's teachers told her that her son had a bad year at school; he was daydreaming and his marks were down. So she spoke to the school counselor, who gave her some reading that explained how divorce is hard on kids and that they need support and guidance. For that year she'd been so busy looking after herself, she missed the fact that she wasn't the only person in the house looking for support.

When parents and children are both hurting, whose needs come first? Many will say that until parents have looked after themselves, they can't care for children. Sounds reasonable, but it's not exactly true. When you get on an airplane, part of the safety lecture is that if the oxygen masks appear, you're to put yours on first and then help children or anyone else who needs assistance. I've heard this analogy used to encourage parents, particularly moms, to look after themselves first. Yes, parents need to look after themselves—but not first.

Children can't wait; they're growing and developing and need our nurturing and attention to allow the maturation process to progress. Adults can wait. We know that we'll have the time to care for ourselves later. The irony of our belief that parents should look after themselves first is that children who need care will act up to get the attention they crave. On the other hand, if we care for them we'll have more time to look after ourselves because our children will behave in healthy ways.

Hannah needed a year and lots of support to recover from the separation and subsequent divorce. And she took it. The children had to wait. Her kids lost a year of healthy development. The research shows that the most important individual factor for a healthy long-term outcome for children of divorce is that both parents continue to actively parent the kids. Hannah's kids missed that. Certainly their day-to-day needs for food and shelter were handled, but their emotional needs were set aside for a while.

Bottom-line: adults must learn to defer their needs and care for the kids first. Parental separation and divorce is hard on everyone, and all parties need care. But the children must come first.

In almost all cases, they're not happy or relieved to see their parents separate and are worried about what will happen to them.

To grow up as independent and self-sufficient young men and women, children need to feel safe and secure throughout their childhood. This safety gives them the freedom to slowly separate from their parents in an appropriate manner.

Issues for Children of Divorce

- The immediate reaction is fear. What's going to happen to me? Who will look after me? If daddy has left, will mommy also leave?
- They're concerned for their parents. Where will daddy live? Will he have a bathroom? (Kids are nothing if not practical!)
- They may be angry. Parents are supposed to make sacrifices for children, not the other way around.
- They often experience loneliness as all supports, including parents, have fallen away.
- There are loyalty conflicts. Who do they support: mommy or daddy?
- Because children see the world through their own eyes, they're likely to assume that this is their fault. If they'd just been good, this wouldn't have happened.
- Children need both parents desperately.

IN OTHER WORDS ...

- We can't protect our children from death, illness or divorce. We can help them learn how to handle themselves when life throws them a curve.
- When bad things happen, we need to be clear with our children about what's going on, and be available to offer them the support they need.
- Look after your children first, then care for your own needs.

TALKING ABOUT BEHAVIOR
Kathy's Q & A

QUESTION

How do I deal with a rebel four-year-old step-child? I've tried almost everything. Please help!

ANSWER

Parenting a step-child carries with it many challenges and frustrations. This four-year-old probably resents your presence in his life. He wants his mom and dad, and he wants them together. Generally, it's preferable to have his biological parent be the primary caregiver and disciplinarian. So try to reduce your parenting role. This will reassure him that you're not trying to take his parent's place.

He may be causing you problems because it's safe. He's not willing to risk the displeasure of his parents because he's afraid of losing them, so you become the target of his fears, insecurities and anger. He needs permission to be angry. Let him express his anger in acceptable ways through physical activity or simply talking about it. But be aware that four-year-olds are quite verbal but not subtle. So, don't take his anger personally; he's angry at the break-up of his family. You're simply the proof that his parents' marriage is over.

How is his relationship with both biological parents, and does he have an ongoing relationship with each? He needs his mother and his father, and his behavior toward you may be a signal that he's feeling the loss of one of his parents. If he has contact with both parents, talk about them, have lots of pictures around and give him permission to talk to you about both his mom and dad.

The issue of love is also a common stumbling block. Because you love the parent, you may believe you should love the child. You don't need to love this child nor does he need to love you. Respect, caring and simple good manners are essential, but love may or may not grow between you. Finally, four-year-olds can be challenging at the best of times. Try to appreciate his energy and give him the time he needs to get to know you.

QUESTION

I'm separated from my daughter who just started grade one. How can I get involved or help her with her schooling over the phone? I'm looking for ideas to get her to tell me about what she's learning.

ANSWER

Keeping in touch with your daughter is the most effective tool you have. She needs to know that, although you're not physically present, you do care about her. This alone will help her learn because she'll be feeling positive about her relationship with you. Asking questions is the most tempting, but usually ineffective, way of getting information from children. In the first place, they don't see their school day as a series of learning experiences, so they're not sure what you want to hear. Some children feel interrogated by questions and are non-responsive. It's much better to just converse and listen. By simply listening to her, you'll start to hear her use new words and phrases and notice that her ability to express herself slowly improves. When you notice her using a new idea or talking about a new skill, you can ask more. Questions such as "What do you like best about adding?" or "Do you have a favorite story?" may encourage discussion.

Stay in touch with the school, too, to find out what's happening. You may want to supplement your phone calls with email or regular mail. Send her books that you can then talk about over the phone. Have her send you some of her schoolwork, which you can assure her is proudly displayed on your fridge. Knowing that you care about her education is the most important gift you can give her.

QUESTION

My daughter is devastated. She just found out she didn't make the elite-level soccer team this year. She's played at this level for three years now (she's ten), and has been with the same group of girls, many of whom did make this year's team. How can I help her get through this major blow to her self-esteem?

ANSWER

While this is a disappointment, it need not be a major blow to her self-esteem. Be careful not to over-react. Let her talk about how she feels, but don't let her wallow in self-pity. Learning how to handle this sort of let-down builds self-esteem as she learns that she can cope with disappointment and get on with her life. One of the downsides of playing at an elite level is that sometimes you don't make the cut. Put the emphasis on her love of the game. She and any of the other girls who didn't make the team can find another place to play. There are many soccer teams around and many community teams don't have try-outs; they simply permit all interested kids to play. Try to be understanding but matter-of-fact and help her find another place to play.

CHAPTER 8

SELF-ESTEEM AND INDEPENDENCE: AN ESSENTIAL PARTNERSHIP

Marjorie is a successful businesswoman and a friend of mine. She walks into a business meeting with an air of authority. When she entertains at home she's gracious and welcoming. And she knows it. She knows her strengths and appreciates them. We'd say that she has high self-esteem. And she does, except in one arena of her life. She has never felt that her family appreciates her. She tells me that she knows her parents and siblings love her, but they don't acknowledge her skills. My guess is that her family would be floored to know this. That's the real challenge of self-esteem. There's a myth that if we love our children they'll know it and will grow to be strong, self-reliant adults with high self-esteem. It's not necessarily so. Whenever I'm speaking to a group and utter the phrase, "I know my mom (or dad) loves me but ..." I see heads nodding all over the room. In my book *Who's In Charge Anyway?* I talked about what we can do to help our children develop high self-esteem. In this book we want to take a look at why that matters. What does it have to do with raising our children to be independent?

WHAT IS SELF-ESTEEM?

In *Who's In Charge Anyway?* I defined self-esteem as my attitude toward myself. When I judge myself as worthy, lovable and capable, I feel I have the capacity to handle whatever life wants to hand me. It's not just liking myself; it's believing in myself and my ability to live my life no matter what the circumstances. It's important for parents to understand the role of self-esteem in helping our children reach independence. Self-esteem can spell the difference between a kid who makes it as a successful adult and one who doesn't.

BUILDING SELF-ESTEEM

Throughout this book we've been looking at how we can help our children become successful adults. By successful I don't mean rich, famous and powerful, although that could happen. I do mean getting on with their lives, making a living, having friends and being happy. Positive self-esteem lets a person of any age know that she can achieve her goals, that she's capable, that she can make it on her own.

TEMPERAMENT

To help our children build a strong sense of ability, we need to reach them. Each child is unique, with his or her own temperament, and each parent is also unique. The more we understand what makes us and our children tick, the more successful we'll be. When we respect our child and his unique personality and respond accordingly, we have a recipe for success. We connect, we click, and our child is responsive to our parenting because we're tuning into his particular mode of communication and connection.

BELONGING

An important piece of the puzzle is a sense of belonging. When we involve our children in doing housework, we let them know that they're needed and belong in a real way to the family. They learn that the family is a working unit that requires the input of all members to make it run well. They learn that they're integral to the process. Without their contribution, things just wouldn't run as smoothly. So, like the toddlers carrying the potatoes in Chapter Five, they can puff out their little chests and know that they matter. Children who have it all done for them never get this wonderful feeling of true belonging. They know that they're present in the family but don't see themselves as having an essential role.

An obvious outcome can be a child who believes in his inherent right to be waited on and have his needs met. But a more subtle result is a sense of inability. The child learns that he's simply not capable; he can't do anything for himself. This sense of incompetence continues throughout his childhood, and once he's reached adulthood he still believes he can't succeed on his own. With that attitude, the likelihood is that he won't succeed. All because we didn't ask him to take out the family garbage!

CONNECTING

Humans are social animals, so we do best when we're connected in healthy ways to other people. Encouraging our children in their relationships with their siblings and friends provides a support system that gives them the strength to move forward. It may seem bizarre to think that the squabbling, bickering relationship your kids have with their siblings is so important to their growth. But remember, working out relationships within the safety of home teaches them how to handle conflict. After all, if they try out every tool they can imagine with their siblings, they'll surely learn what does and doesn't work. Actually, it's interesting to watch our children. They may call each other the most appalling names, and shriek insults at each other that make your hair curl, but let an outsider insult a sibling and the gloves are off. Suddenly these same kids join together in support against the rest of the world.

Connecting with friends has the same sort of outcome but without the intensity found in sibling relationships. Friends provide a support system that permits risk. A certain amount of risk-taking is essential if kids are to make it on their own. When we think of risk, we think of going over Niagara Falls in a barrel. For kids, though, it might be going into the corner store to buy gum. It's much easier to do it with a friend. Each step toward independence feels risky for kids, but if we let them make the steps and encourage their friendships, the journey to self-reliance will run more smoothly. Friends also look after and protect each other, making it safer for them to move slowly away from the sphere of adult influence into the outside world.

BEING CAPABLE

Feeling capable and being capable are what it's all about. Being capable means either knowing how to do something or being confident in your ability to learn. Being capable means being self-reliant and growing up to be successful. We started this book talking about play. At first that seems like a strange topic to cover. But that's where it starts. Through healthy play children learn how to make things work and how to explore ideas. Play is research, it's experimentation. And it helps children feel capable and able to figure out the world around them. When we expect our children to play a role in the running of our household, we let them know that we trust in their ability to perform a given task that's necessary to our well-being and quality of life. When two-year-old Jeremy puts the spoons on the table, then sees us use those very spoons to eat our soup, he knows that he made it possible for us to have dinner. He's certainly a capable person.

It's often during the most difficult times that our children learn the most. If we try to protect a child from the reality of whatever is happening, he'll get the message that we don't think he's capable. By letting him know what's really happening, and why his parents are upset or anxious, we tell him that he's capable of sharing the family problems as well as the triumphs. Of course, we involve him only as far as is appropriate for his age, and we reassure him that we'll look after him, but we tell him the truth rather than pretend there's nothing going on. He knows things aren't right in the house and being included benefits his development.

Letting a child take control of aspects of her own life also leads to a genuine feeling of capability. The toddler who's given time to struggle out of his own socks and pants before his bath, the pre-schooler who dresses herself each morning, the school-age child who chooses his own clothes and the teen who manages a clothing allowance are all taking control of their own lives at a level appropriate to their age.

TELLING OR DEMONSTRATING: WHICH WORKS?

Over the years there's been a trend towards telling people they're great so that they'll believe they're great and thus develop high self-esteem. If only it were that easy! Self-esteem is built through adversity, through success, through effort and through responding to challenges. That doesn't mean you have to be perfect to develop high self-esteem, but it does mean you have to work at it.

Five-year-old Tyler comes into the living room after struggling for the past five minutes to tie his shoelaces. He's beaming; he did it, and let me tell you it wasn't easy. He feels great about himself. If you had simply tied his shoes for him and told him he was terrific he wouldn't beam. It may not even register, particularly if he hears that all the time but never gets to experience hard work and success. Think about the look on a baby's face when she actually takes her first step. This is after days or weeks of pulling herself up on the furniture, falling on her well-padded bottom, moving around carefully, hanging onto the coffee table and chairs. One look at her face and you know all the work, all the falls, all the failures were worth it. She doesn't need anyone to tell her she's terrific! You certainly should add your excitement, though, as your pleasure in her success is the icing on the cake.

What's your proudest accomplishment? I bet you had to work hard to achieve it and the harder it was, the better you felt. Could someone telling you that you're the greatest replace that feeling? No way. Prove it, you'd want to say. But if you struggled to reach a goal, you don't need anyone to tell you. You know. It's so easy to do everything for your children because you can, because you want to, because it feels good. And it does. But responsible parents look past that and let their kids take control when they're ready, then watch with pleasure as they become increasingly independent and self-reliant along with high self-esteem.

IN OTHER WORDS ...

- It's really all about self-esteem. When kids feel connected and capable they're able to move confidently to independence.
- All the ideas and skills mentioned in this book will help children develop high self-esteem.

TALKING ABOUT BEHAVIOR
Kathy's Q & A

QUESTION
My nine-year-old wants to go trick-or-treating around the neighborhood with her best friend without adult accompaniment. I think she's too young and this is unsafe. What should I do?

ANSWER
For children, Halloween is a wonderful holiday and quite unlike any other. They get to be out after dark, dress in strange and spooky outfits, go from house to house and collect goodies. It's slightly scary, exciting and fun. But, for parents, Halloween has become a frightening ritual. We're nervous about stranger abduction, about traffic and about the safety of the goodies our children get. In many communities, parents have replaced the traditional Halloween ritual with community center parties. For most children this just isn't the same thing. Halloween is unique and should be a positive experience for our children. The trick is to make it safe without ruining it.

Young children are happy to have their parents walk with them. Slightly older children (six to eight) will accept their parent's company as long as it's subtle. But by nine or ten, they want parents to stay home. Generally, I believe we should let children nine years old and older go out without us. However, it's probably best to have a bigger group of kids rather than just the two little girls.

And we need to develop some guidelines. The first is that they should have friends we trust to go out with them. Talk to the other parents so that the children have the same limits and expectations. Determine their route by considering your neighborhood and traffic patterns. Ask the children to bring all the goodies home to be checked over by parents before they eat them. And let them know they should approach only houses with outside lights turned on. Finally, plan a route that has the children check in at home part way through their walk. Then let them go, and trust that they'll handle it and have fun.

QUESTION

We seem to be at a watershed over after-school care for our eleven-year-old. He's balking at having a babysitter for the couple of hours until we get home from work. But is it a good idea to leave him alone at this age? Please advise.

ANSWER

They don't call this age group the "tweens" for nothing. They're too old for babysitters and too young to babysit. It's a real dilemma for parents.

There isn't a hard-and-fast rule for this age group. Look at a number of considerations. Consider your child's level of responsibility. Some eleven-year-olds are pretty level-headed while others are still impulsive. If you've left him for short periods with no problems, you'll feel more comfortable letting him be home alone after school. Look at how he handles coming into an empty house and staying by himself. Are there are other people nearby he can call if he needs help? The length of time and how frequently he'll be alone are issues. If he has extracurricular activities one or two afternoons a week, that will make it easier.

Children also need to socialize, so you may want to consider allowing him to have a friend over whom you know well. Speaking of that, you need to be clear with him if he needs permission before he has a friend over. Once you decide that he can look after himself, it's important to develop some guidelines. Some issues to consider are whether he should contact you after school, how he'll look after the house key, what to say when answering the phone and door, whether you expect him to do chores and who he can call for help. Then give it a month and reassess.

QUESTION

I'd like to send our two daughters (aged eight-and-a-half and ten) to overnight camp this summer. They're refusing, and I know they'd never go on their own initiative. Is it wise to send them when they claim not to be interested, or is it okay to give them a little nudge? I feel they'll like it and have a great time once they're settled.

ANSWER

The best way to prepare children for summer camp is to ease them into it. Begin with overnight stays with family, and then with friends. Once they've become accustomed to sleeping away from mom and dad for one night it gets easier. There are many short camps for beginners. They last about three days and give children a chance to have the experience without the longer week or two-week stay. Some children find it much more fun to go with someone they know, so if the two girls are going together they may feel more at ease. On the other hand, you may find that your ten-year-old is ready to go, but her younger sister needs another year. In that case respect their different developmental levels; have the younger girl wait a year, and recruit a friend to go with your ten-year-old.

Another way to interest children in camp is to do the research and find one that really sparks their interest. Whether it's computers, soccer, chess, horseback riding or water sports, if the camp offers activities that the kids love, they're more likely to want to attend. If they're truly adamant that they don't want to go, relax and try again next year.

CHAPTER 9

'TWIXT TWELVE AND TWENTY: THOSE PESKY TEEN YEARS

One day it happens: a little girl kisses you goodnight and heads off to bed. The next morning, she appears at the breakfast table and she's different. She looks like your little girl except, well, she's wearing some makeup. Not much, just a bit of lipstick and mascara, but makeup nonetheless. And when you wish her good morning, she grunts. Where is your chipper little Miss? Parents of teens will tell you that it seems kids become teenagers overnight. They develop an attitude, are fixated on their looks and spend hours chatting either online or on the phone with their friends. And suddenly you're no longer the source of all wisdom. Some fourteen-year-old with acne and a cracking voice is the expert on everything and you, my friend, are the older generation.

Throughout this book we've been talking about how our parenting choices help our children to reach independence. The difference is this: before puberty we know it's important, but we believe we have all the time in the world. Now they're teens and it's real and it's immediate. This is it, the final leg of the journey we're taking with our children to their maturity. It's pretty simple to talk about the role of play in the development of autonomy when the child is a toddler playing with blocks. But what about when he's at a party on the other side of town with kids you don't even know? No question, the goals are the same, but the road is rockier for both parent and teen.

DISCIPLINE

Teens not only need discipline, they want it. Really. However, discipline takes on a different flavor with teens, as compared to their younger selves. We can distract or move a toddler when he's about to get into trouble, but a teen needs to be involved and engaged in the family's discipline decisions. With teens it's important to be prepared to negotiate the boundaries. First, you need to be absolutely clear on your bottom line. It's like going to an auction. If you arrive and think that you'll decide how much to spend as you go along, you'll leave with stuff but no money. You can get caught up in the action. So you need to determine how much you can spend in advance. When you sit down with your teen to determine the new expanded rules that recognize his age, you need to know what you're prepared to negotiate and which rules are set in stone.

Of course, what's set in stone for a thirteen-year-old will be different for an eighteen-year-old. While your young teen will start to go further afield, like taking the bus downtown, she still needs permission and to inform you of all her travel plans: where she's going, who with and when she'll be home. By eighteen she'll let you know her plans but not need permission. However, there will still be a bottom-line rule about no drinking and driving. It can be challenging because the teen years cover such a span of development. A thirteen-year-old is still a child on the cusp of adolescence and seems to move back and forth from the child she was to the teen she's becoming. By eighteen this same teen is a young adult, at least most of the time!

So it's a process that takes you from the increasing independence of your young teen to the day your teen leaves home to start her life as an independent young adult. Young adults today tend to leave home at a later age than in previous generations, but the need for independence remains. In the next chapter we'll talk not only about leaving home but also, about the importance of treating your kids as independent young adults no matter where they live. At any rate, once you've determined your bottom line, you can negotiate the rules and expectations with your teen, working together to set the family expectations.

Teens need rules and they need input. Rules give them the security of knowing the limits. Adolescence is a time of surging emotions. Their hormones are taking over: they can be as impulsive as two-year-olds and sometimes, it seems, as irresponsible. Rules will help them curb their impulsive selves. Friends and friendships play an increasing role in their lives, and this can lead to peer pressure. Peer pressure is simply kids being influenced by other kids. We see it as negative when we see teens making really dumb decisions to follow other kids. You ask your teen, "Why did you skip class?" and the response is something like, "I don't know. Hayden said we should. It seemed like a good idea at the time." Those are the times you're tempted to say, "If all the kids were going to jump off a bridge would you follow?"

Rules give teens the chance to say they can't go along with the crowd because there's this dumb family rule about attending classes. Then they can blame you and save a little face with their friends. I want to make the point, though, that peer pressure isn't always a bad thing. Kids join debating clubs and soccer teams, learn to play guitar and find part-time work because of their friends' recommendations. They develop new interests and broaden their ideas through contact with new friends. Bottom line, rules reassure them that you do care enough to set the standards for their behavior. This gives them a feeling of security, which can help them develop a good sense of self and lead them to believe in themselves and their abilities, and thus move toward independence.

TRUST AND LETTING GO

I remember the first time my daughter went downtown with a girlfriend. We had talked about it and knew that she was ready. But when the time came for her to leave, I felt panicky and said to her, "I'm not sure I'm ready for this." Her response was: "It's okay, Mom, you haven't been quite ready for every new step I've taken, but you catch up real quick." Of course, she survived and so did I. I needed to let her go and simply wait and trust that she was okay and would come home happy and healthy.

The irony is that our expectations of our kids actually help them move to independence. As they roam further afield, the guidelines we've set help them to learn to pay attention to where they are and what other considerations they need to take into account. For example, while they're out with their friends having fun, they still need to be aware of the time and when they should start back to make it home on time. This has the long-term effect of helping them learn that no matter how much they're enjoying themselves, they need to be aware of their other responsibilities. Once they're on their own and not answerable to us, they'll be able to use this experience to make responsible decisions.

And yes, they'll make mistakes. Some of the mistakes they make we'll hear about—if they dawdle after the movie and miss the bus, for example. Some we'll never know about. For instance, they may go to a party that gets out of hand, and they know they shouldn't stay, but they do. That's not a choice you hope your child will make, but one he might. He'll make some bad choices, and he'll learn from them whether we ever find out about them or not.

Think back, and I'm sure you'll remember some poor decisions you made, and learned from, when you were a teen. We'd like to protect our kids from these errors but can't, so we need to be there, to trust them and, yes, we can worry. They can move toward independence from the safety of home while you're there to help, support and guide them, or they can learn when they're totally on their own with no safety net. Cell phones have gone a long way to creating parental peace of mind. We know that if our kids need us, they can call, without having to depend on the availability of a pay phone. If your child has a cell phone, it shouldn't be seen as a lifeline allowing you to check in on your sixteen-year-old every hour on the hour. We need to trust our teens. They need us to trust them.

Teen independence requires getting to where they're going and home again on their own. But it doesn't mean total freedom. Throughout their teens, our kids are moving at what feels like breakneck speed to independence. And that's the way it should feel, but that isn't the way it should really be. There are still ground rules. We don't need to have GPS locators to keep tabs on them every minute of the day, but we do need to know where they're going, when they'll be home and how they're going to be traveling.

CHORES

As we discussed in Chapter Five, chores give our kids a role in the the family and teach them that running a household requires the work and cooperation of all family members. In adolescence, chores have an additional and essential role to play. Chores teach kids how to look after themselves. After all, it's pretty hard to be independent if you haven't a clue how to collect and take out the garbage, run a washing machine or cook dinner.

At this point you need to look at the chores your kids do, think about the skills they'll need when they move out and assess the gaps. Then develop a plan to expand the range of chores they do around the house. I know they have a busy schedule, but they need to learn how to care for themselves. Fitting household chores into a busy life is an essential skill these days. On the other hand, be realistic. Rotate chores so that your child is learning all that he needs to know without becoming a slave to the house-work. If you have been holding regular family meetings, this is the best place to develop a weekly schedule that includes chores for the week. With teens, it's time to have a mix of daily chores like dishes and picking up in the living room, weekly chores like laundry and taking out the garbage, and occasional special tasks like painting the fence.

Now, let's not kid ourselves, our teens aren't going to rise to these challenges with pleasure and excitement, all the while thanking us for giving them the opportunity to gain these lifelong skills. So first we need to make sure they know what they're doing. No matter how simple the task, they need to learn how to do it.

Teen Tasks

Besides the chores included in the list in Chapter Five, teens need to take charge of day-to-day tasks. These are jobs that you should hand over to your teen one at a time. And all jobs should be taught to both boys and girls,

Laundry

Fourteen-year-old Jack needs to learn how the dirty clothing that he tosses in his hamper magically turns up clean and ironed in his closet.

Cooking

One evening a week it's your teen's turn to cook dinner for the family. That includes menu planning, cooking more than one dish (so a boxed macaroni and cheese just doesn't cut it) and bringing the nutritious meal hot to the table.

Yard Work

It's time to introduce your child to the lawn mower, rakes and snow shovel. Teach her not only how to do the yard work but also how to care for and maintain the tools and equipment.

Housework

Until now your kids may have had to load the dishwasher or vacuum the living room. It's time for them to understand the big picture. Now, I'm not suggesting that they suddenly start cleaning the whole house on a regular basis. But they do need to know how; and that includes being involved in discussions about what needs doing this week and why.

Repairs

Involve your kids when doing household repairs, including everything from changing a light bulb to dry-walling the new addition. At the very least, basic tools like screwdrivers, hammers and plungers should be familiar to them.

As I've already mentioned, it's always a neat idea to work with your kids. With teens this is particularly true for the bigger jobs. They'll also need reminding and supervising. Doing chores just isn't the most important thing on their radar screen so you'll likely need to get involved in making it happen. A deadline helps: "This needs to be done by dinner time Saturday," or "The garbage gets picked up first thing Tuesday morning, so you need to get it out before bed on Monday." Our goal is to make sure our kids have the skills they need to get on with their lives, as well as developing time management skills.

THE FAMILY CAR

A huge sign of independence is a driver's license. Teens aspire to it, but not all parents share their dream. However, it's likely going to happen sooner or later so it's best to think about the consequences. The first step is lessons. High-quality lessons are the best way to start the process, but they can be costly. So, consider making the lessons a birthday gift. The rules for obtaining a license vary across the country so you'll need to do a bit of research to find out how things work in your area.

The challenging part comes after she gets her license. Now what? This is when the discussion about insurance raises its ugly head. In some provinces they insure drivers, with younger drivers paying a premium, and in others, such as British Columbia where I live, they insure vehicles. You'll have to decide about insurance. Will your teen pay his own premium; is it a gift or will you share the cost? In our house, because our cars were already insured, it wasn't an issue. However, the kids were clear that if they had an accident that was their fault, they would paid the increased insurance costs for as many years as it took for it to return to the regular rate.

Make sure you set some expectations about gas; otherwise you might be in for a major inconvenience when you jump into a car with the needle hovering way below empty and the warning light in full color. It's fair to ask them to put gas in the car whenever they take it any distance and to ask their friends to pitch in and help. Scheduling car use becomes an agenda item for family meetings. Planning ahead prevents the arguments and disappointments that are sure to arise. And having a licensed driver in the house is great. No longer do you have to drive to every soccer practice (you can still go to the games to cheer) and when you need something from the store, there's a keener ready to run any errand you name. I also found it reassuring knowing that my child had reliable transport home when she was out in the evening.

You do need to address the issue of drinking and driving. Fortunately, most of our youth are more responsible than we were, but we know that not only are there still kids driving cars when they're impaired, but there are also passengers traveling with them. Let your kids know that you'll come and get them any time they need a ride home from anywhere. Some families have cab fare easily available that their teens can grab as soon as they arrive home. This is a great option, as you may not always be home, or they may have the family car, making it impossible for you to go get them. If your teens are heading to a party in the country, brainstorm some options for safe travel home.

MONEY MANAGEMENT

Children's allowances are generally seen as being used for treats, recreation and school lunches. With teens, we're into a whole new area of finances. Their recreational and extracurricular spending needs are growing as fast as they are, and their clothing is more expensive (no one warns you that a teen wears adult sizes at adult prices and outgrows them in less than a year). I'm a great believer in giving both a standard allowance and also a clothing allowance once your child is a teenager. You may decide he's not ready until his fourteenth or fifteenth birthday, but it's a great learning experience for your teen. He has to decide how to make his money stretch, and that's it. There are some fabulous benefits to this system. One is that you're no longer fighting with him about what to buy. If he wants very expensive brand-name jeans, then he only gets one pair, and that's his problem. And as he's doing his own laundry, not having as many clothing options is also his problem. Another interesting benefit is that when you buy him underwear and socks for Christmas he's thrilled; until this clothing allowance, he never had any idea how much these simple basics cost.

One wrinkle I need to mention is growth spurts. You may find that suddenly, none of your son's clothing fits, as he's grown two inches and put on twenty pounds. This is very common when teens change from their summer wardrobe to fall school outfits. In our house, this called for a "growth bonus": extra money to cover the problem. We also helped with big purchases like coats and boots. But even though you're ponying up extra cash, your teen is aware of how much everything costs.

Teens are also interested in earning extra money. They generally start by babysitting or doing yard work in the neighborhood and move quickly to the part-time jobs available to teens on evenings and weekends. This work teaches kids valuable lessons. Suddenly, they're working for someone who isn't interested in excuses or their other interests. They either show up on time and do the work, or get fired. Simple. Part-time work is great for teens as long as it doesn't take over their life. Twelve hours a week is plenty for a high school student. When they work too many hours, their schoolwork suffers, they're likely to become sleep-deprived and they drop their high school friends to spend more time at work. They can also find earning money very enticing and end up with more cash in their pocket than is really good for them. It's important to remember that their primary goal is to graduate high school, and that has to take precedence.

SNOOPING

Adolescence can be so rocky for both teens and parents. Teenagers just don't tell us everything the way they did when they were younger. In addition, the trouble they can get into is much more serious than when they were little. Drugs, AIDS, pregnancy—the list goes on and on, and we're so worried. It's easy to justify a little precautionary snooping just to make sure our kids are okay. We want to go through their drawers, read their email, open any letters and check out their diaries. *Don't!* It's an invasion of privacy, and the minute your child realizes that you've been snooping, any hope you had of reaching her is lost or at least is in serious jeopardy. A big aspect to trust is staying out of their private lives. Trust is the basis of respect, and respect is the basis for any important relationship.

IN OTHER WORDS ...

- Adolescence is the final leg in the journey toward independence.
- Our teens need both discipline and our support. However, the style changes to reflect their increased maturity.
- One of the goals of having them do chores and learn to manage money is to prepare them to be capable adults.

TALKING ABOUT BEHAVIOR
Kathy's Q & A

QUESTION

My thirteen-year-old has such an active social life he's never home. While I like all his friends and activities, I'd also like him to have time for family meals and chores. How can we work this out?

ANSWER

Balancing home life and social life can be tough for families of teens. Children your son's age need to gain independence, and they do this by forming strong friendships. Peers take on an increasingly central role in their lives, sometimes at the expense of family and household responsibilities. But these kids still have to learn to save some time for the family. Sit down with your son and plan times when he'll be home to eat with the family and pitch in with chores. He needs to hear from you that you expect him to be home for meals a certain number of times a week and that he has to do his share of the housework; however, he can choose when he'll do these things.

Family meetings are a very effective way to handle this planning. The whole family sits down together on a regular basis (weekly often works best) to organize schedules and chores and to discuss any problems or concerns. It's important that you establish this pattern now so that as your son gets into his teens, the habit of staying connected to family will be in place. It's great that you like your son's friends; by all means invite them over to join you for family meals and activities. This will make staying home more attractive.

QUESTION

I have five children and my eldest is twelve. I find she doesn't tell me a whole lot about what's going on in her life. It's very hard to communicate with her. She says she has a boyfriend, and I'd like to talk with her about it, but she thinks I'm being nosy. How can I get her to open up?

ANSWER

Most children go through a private stage at about twelve or thirteen. They whisper on the phone, go straight to their rooms with their friends for long secret conversations and shrug off all your questions. So, for starters, she's typical. The best way to handle this stage is to respect her privacy but be available when she does want to talk. She'll view your questions as interrogation. The trick is simply to listen. The more you listen, the more she'll talk. You also want to check out the terms she uses. Having a boyfriend may mean something quite different for her than for you. So you can say, "When I was your age, you know when dinosaurs roamed the earth, having a boyfriend meant … is it the same today?" I remember my daughter saying to me that her friend was "going out" with Dennis. Well, I assumed that meant they were going on a date. She explained it meant being a couple. So, in my lexicon, they were going steady. There are also young teens who talk about having a boyfriend, and while they do like each other, the relationship outside of school is limited to phone calls or MSN. It's important that you get to know her friends. The best way is to become a driver. Drive groups of kids to soccer practice, to the mall or school dances. And make your home a comfortable haven for her and her friends. Let them listen to their music and serve lots of snacks.

QUESTION

I have an eleven-year-old step-daughter. Her mother and I disagree about her wearing eye makeup and lipstick. Is she too young?

ANSWER

Parenting step-children requires extreme tact when you disagree with the parent. The rule of thumb is that the biological parent makes the decisions. I believe it's just fine to let her mother know how you feel. But, once you've done that, you should leave it to mother and daughter to work out. Respect the decision that her mother makes. Getting into an argument with either your step-daughter or her mother over this issue isn't helpful. But remember, makeup or not, she's still a little girl. That being said, there isn't a magic age for wearing makeup. It varies not only from town to town but also school to school. Take a look at her friends and see what they're wearing. At eleven, makeup is probably not appropriate for school, but a little light lip-gloss is fine. Most of the kids I see are wearing glitter on their eyes, lips or cheeks. Wearing makeup is quite a rite of passage for some girls. The trick is for the makeup to be appropriate for her age and the occasion. Fortunately, there's a wide range of pale pastel colors available for her. So, if you'll be making decisions when she's with you, sit down with her and her Dad, and make some decisions about what she can wear for special occasions.

QUESTION

I recently moved in with the love of my life who lives eight hundred kilometers from my hometown. Both my children love him very much, although my fourteen-year-old stayed behind, and to this day, is still against moving in with all of us. He says his life is in our hometown and doesn't even want to think about moving. I need him in my life (as I keep telling him). I know I'm his mother and I do have full custody, but then I keep hearing from family that I shouldn't force or push him to move far away from our hometown.

ANSWER

It's understandable that a fourteen-year-old wouldn't want to move. All teens want to stay put. He has a right to his feelings, but he's a child and needs to come with you. He doesn't have to like it, but you're his parent and you make the final decisions about where he'll live. It isn't just that you need him in your life (which you do). It's that he needs parenting, and you're his parent. He may surprise himself by discovering that he can actually be happy and develop a life in a new place.

I notice that you also refer to your last home as your hometown. You need to model making this new location your home. Together you can discover the joys of a new location. Perhaps your partner would like to help you both explore the sights and sounds of your new home. Every day teens move with their parents owing to job changes, new opportunities or new relationships. And they survive quite nicely. He can stay in touch with his friends by mail (either email or snail mail). He may also be able to visit them in the summer.

Chapter 10

WHAT DO YOU MEAN I CAN'T LIVE HERE FOREVER?

"I see now that learning to be a mother was child's play compared to learning to be a not-mother. Making sure she's okay comes right after breathing in my hierarchy of needs. Suddenly, now I'm required (by her developmental calendar, not mine) to stop paying that kind of attention to her. Having children is hard, but letting them go is much harder, an emotional amputation. My new job, which I didn't choose, is to open my eyes to her wings and watch her fly; to set her free and trust that she'll be fine, that she'll make the life she needs. Having never been on her own, she requires life skills that aren't in her kit bag yet. There's only one way to get them: the hard way. Without me there to smooth the bumps, I'm scared for her. "

Joanne Kates, who's the director of Camp Arowhon in Algonquin Park and restaurant critic for the *Globe and Mail*, wrote this as part of an article about a trip she took with her eighteen-year-old daughter to Europe. I couldn't have said it better myself. This is what it's all about. We become parents, and the job takes over our life. We worry, we laugh, we comfort, we discipline and teach, and then we let them go. Our baby is now ready to leave the nest, and we have to stay behind and wave goodbye.

My friend Brenda told me that leaving home for her was actually quite simple. You see, she's one of the older children of a big family (twelve kids) and it was expected that as each child graduated high school, he or she would move on, making room for a younger sibling. She didn't feel rejected; it was a fact of life, and she'd grown up knowing it. I have other friends who were anxious to leave so that they could have their own bedroom as they'd always shared a room with at least one other sibling. And yes, some looked forward to having sex with their boyfriend or girlfriend. Okay, that was the reality for those of us growing up in the '50s, and it's not the case today. Fair enough, but our children still have to grow up, become independent and start to live their own lives. We expect that they will become independent adults. We need to prepare them to do so and to believe that they can do it. The good news is, when we let them go, they often come back for a visit. They stay connected.

POSTSECONDARY EDUCATION AND LETTING GO

At the beginning of the school year, there are always stories in the media about kids starting school. But lately there's a new trend in the regular early September crop of stories about preparing your kids for kindergarten and choosing the right high school. These are stories about young adults who have graduated from high school and been accepted into institutions of higher learning.

Two stood out for me this year. One was the story of a first-year university student registering for classes and struggling to get the courses he wanted. So far, a pretty typical scene. However, he wasn't speaking for himself. He was one of a number of students with a parent in tow, doing all the talking. My goodness, it's bad enough when registering an eight-year-old for grade three and speaking on his behalf as if he doesn't know his name and birthday and what school he attended last year, but a university student! What's going on here? Sure, registering for college or university and getting the courses you want is challenging, but it's a challenge that any young person who made it to this level can, and should, handle on his own. The second story was about the parent of a young adult in first-year university who hadn't heard from him in three days. So she called the director of her son's residence to have him call home. How inappropriate! How embarrassing for the student!

The stories are legion: parents phoning to see if their kids are attending classes, showing up at frosh events, hassling the professors about workload and marks. It would be funny if it weren't all too true. You've done your job; now let them go. You are still and will always be their parent, but the relationship must change. Just think about any time your parents interfered in your adult life. How did you feel?

LIVING AT HOME

Eighteen-year-old Geoffrey lives at home. He has a job in a fast food restaurant and is looking for better paying work. On payday, he sits down with his parents and writes them a cheque for twenty-five percent of his gross income. His parents taught him that once he's no longer a student, he must pay his own way. However, they realize that, until he can find a better job, he'll find it difficult to live on his own, so they've agreed that he'll live at home and cover the cost or room and board. He's also expected to pull his own weight by helping out around the house, cooking some meals, doing his own laundry and doing his share of house-work and yard work. His parents treat him as an adult who lives with them. He no longer has a curfew but is expected to let them know if he'll be away overnight or away for dinner. That, they say, is only good manners when you live together.

In some ways, having a young adult living at home is like having a boarder in the home. Your child is now an independent person paying rent. On the other hand, he's still your child, and you'll want to figure out your expectations for him. I believe that he should be expected to help out around the house with chores, cooking and yard work, as well as taking care of his own laundry and the cleanliness of his own room. (I believe that all kids should get to determine the state of their room, as long as the mess doesn't spill out into the rest of the house.) Guests are another issue. Having friends over for dinner is one thing, but what about having a girlfriend spend the night? These are questions you need to discuss and answer, based on your values and your child's age. Talk about them ahead of time so that you all know where you stand.

If your twenty-something child is living at home, you all need to make the transition from a child living at home to an adult living with you. If you cater to his every need you're not helping him grow up. Often, when I speak to parents of young adults, they tell me stories of an eighteen, nineteen or twenty-year-old who lives at home, pays no rent and does no chores. What, they ask, should they do? Simple. Set out the expectations. Let them know the rules. You do your young adult no favors when you let him freeload. Why should anyone leave home if they have their own bedroom, a full fridge, someone to cook, do laundry and clean house, and there's even space for them to invite their friends in for a visit? I've also spoken to parents who've saved the rent money they collected from their child and invested it in a tuition account. This is a great idea, particularly if your child has decided to work for a year before heading off for more education or training. But what about a young adult living at home and attending some postsecondary education or training?

In our house, the rule was that if they were attending school they paid no rent but were expected to pull their weight doing chores. We told them about this rule when they were in high school so it would come as no surprise. The question of living at home while going to university, college, an apprentice program or the like is a dicey one. On the one hand, it's become extremely expensive to continue with an education after high school. On the other hand, it's more difficult for a young person to forge a separate adult identity while living in the family home. Of course, many of you are jumping up and down wanting to point out that there are hundreds of towns that have no postsecondary institutions and their young people have no choice but to live away from home.

Given a choice, I recommend that a young person move out of the family home and learn how to live on their own, making choices away from the watching eyes of their parents. I remember speaking to Maureen, a young woman studying art at the Emily Carr Institute in Vancouver. She had grown up in Ottawa and told me that she found it hard to discover her true adult identity while staying in her hometown. She said that everyone who had known her all her life had expectations of how she'd behave and act, and that any attempt she made to explore new ideas or activities was extremely difficult.

I also speak to parents who don't want their children to have to live in less than perfect conditions. They believe that their kids should live at home until they're able to move into a three-bedroom house with new furniture. But once an adult child can pay the rent for a basement suite or shared apartment and buy some used furniture, it's time for her to spread her wings. I suggest to these parents that they remember their own first place, whether it was a room in residence, a basement suite or a house shared with four or five other young people. Sure, it was probably awful, but most of us recall our first place fondly. I had the standard board and brick bookshelves. My trunk, emptied of all my worldly belongings, served nicely as a coffee table and the living room couch doubled as my bed. My roommate won the toss and got the single bed in the tiny bedroom. Mind you, she had to put up with me wandering through her room to the microscopic bathroom. It was tiny, old, awful and OURS, and we loved it.

Part of growing up is moving from the grungy and fabulous first place to increasingly better places and being able to look back and see your progress. Young adults who live at home should be clear why they're still living with their parents and when and under what conditions they'll become independent.

THEIR FIRST APARTMENT

Whether they leave home to go to school or to get on with their lives, they'll need to find a place to live. Many students spend their first year in residence, which is a great transition from their parents' home to their own home. However, many others (like both of mine) don't. For students who need to find a place to live there's usually some sort of bulletin board or housing office at the school with affordable listings as well as opportunities for finding roommates. Whether your child is a student or employed, at some point she'll be looking for a place to live.

So what's the line between supporting your child in this venture and taking over? This is a huge step for your child, and she'll likely appreciate the support, as long as she's driving the process. For example, if she comes home and finds you've circled some great places in the newspaper and set up appointments to view, that's taking over. If you offer to look through the paper with her and join her when she goes to look at places, that's support. Offer support, answer her questions and suggest things she should consider, like finding out the rental rules in your province so that she understands her rights and responsibilities as a tenant. Lend her your truck if you have one and offer the old couch from the family room. After she moves in, go over with a casserole or pizza. But then, remember, this is her home. Don't snoop, show up unannounced, or come over and do her laundry. She's an adult. But do be available with advice if she asks; after all this is her first place, and she's likely to have some questions

It's easy to say that our children need certain skills before they head off on their own. But what are they? They need to be able to manage time and money, do basic housework, shop and cook. They need to deal with landlords and roommates and, if necessary, plumbers or electricians. There are many new skills they'll develop along the way, but there are some basics that will make the transition from dependent child to independent adult relatively painless.

Throughout this book we've been setting the scene for this moment, the moment we let go and they find their own way. They won't know everything they need to know before they leave; but they'll have enough experience to figure it out. For example, they learned that to see a movie they need to determine when the show starts and what bus will get them to the theatre on time. Then they learned to figure out all the costs involved, and to organize the outing with friends. It's not a huge jump to the bigger playing field of taking a bus, train or plane to another city and of considering all the dynamics of such a trip. When you send them to the store to pick up some groceries, they have to figure out the basics of navigating the store, finding what they need and even paying some attention to the cost. Well, probably not the latter. After all, it's your money, not theirs. But it's a start.

As I said in *Who's In Charge Anyway?*, if we model, expect, demand and supervise the standards of our children's behavior, we'll have taken on the responsibility of parenting our kids. And wi'll give them security—the roots children need to grow into

What Kids Need to Know When They Leave Home

First Challenges

We've already discussed housework, so let's just say that they need to know how to keep their home as neat as they and their roommates wish. Besides the basics, there are other skills they need. Take the test. Does your child either have these skills or the know-how to acquire them?

Accommodation

[ ] Finding an apartment, plus determining "going rate" and affordability, assessing locations, using want ads/student housing offices, understanding added costs (heat, hydro, parking) or details on utilities

[ ] Signing a lease

[ ] Communicating with landlord about problems

[ ] Furnishing/equipping on a budget

[ ] Arranging phone, gas, hydro, cable and Internet service (if no credit history, may require a deposit)

[ ] Finding roommates

[ ] Negotiating cooking/cleaning and partying schedules with roommates (a big challenge when you're on different schedules, for example shift workers)

Basic maintenance

[ ] Changing fuses

[ ] Indoor painting

[ ] Hanging blinds/curtains/pictures

[ ] Arranging insurance on contents and/or any valuables

Money management

[ ] Setting up a bank account

[ ] Writing cheques

[ ] Using an ATM

[ ] Budgeting

[ ] Paying the bills

[ ] Negotiating shared expenses with roommates

[ ] For students, applying for scholarships, loans and bursaries

[ ] Handling student loans including payment deferrals

Transportation

[ ] Understanding transit maps and schedules

[ ] Pumping gas

[ ] Routine car maintenance (e.g., oil change, topping up fluids—DIY or scheduling mechanic visits)

[ ] Maintaining adequate insurance/licensing

Eating and drinking

[ ] Menu planning

[ ] Grocery shopping (within a budget)

[ ] Cooking and safe food storage

Work and study skills

[ ] Handling self in a job interview

[ ] Writing a resume

[ ] Appropriate dress

[ ] Punctuality

[ ] Time management: prioritizing and balancing work and play

Personal

[ ] Basic health care

[ ] Finding a doctor, dentist, etc.

[ ] Making friends

Panic phone calls home

Once they've been away for a while, you'll hear from them. They'll have questions about the following:

[ ] How to locate water and gas shut-off valves

[ ] How to unclog sinks and toilets

[ ] How to do laundry at the laundromat

[ ] Entertaining ("Mom, how do you cook a roast?")

Even later they may want to discuss the following:

[ ] How to negotiate a bank loan

[ ] Saving money: RRSPs, vacation fund, cushion in case of unemployment

[ ] How to file income tax

[ ] Business networking skills

[ ] First house purchase

And so on, right on to their own child's first case of croup and beyond.

healthy young men and women. Then we give them wings. We prepare them for independence. We expect that they'll become independent, and we believe in their ability to handle their own lives.

IN OTHER WORDS ...

• Letting go of our children isn't easy. But it's our job.
• As our children grow we're preparing them for independence.
• It's our responsibility to ensure that they have the basic skills they need to live as adults.

TALKING ABOUT BEHAVIOR
Kathy's Q & A

QUESTION

Why are young adults today so reluctant to move out of the family home?

ANSWER

The question concerns a change in focus. Those who grew up in the '50s and '60s could hardly wait to move out. One of the reasons was that many of us were sharing a bedroom with at least one other sibling, and we wanted our own space. Today, staying home means having your own room, a full fridge, access to a car, computer, and laundry facilities—the good life.

Another obvious consideration is the increased cost of housing as a renter or owner. If you're fortunate enough to live in a town that has the postsecondary institution of your choice, it's certainly cheaper to live at home. For some reason, previous generations of children were more highly motivated to get out and have their "own" life. Maybe the generation gap today isn't as wide. Many young people today have more choices and freedom while growing up, so they don't feel they need to get out of the family home. Remaining at home can lead to tension, however, as the young adult wants to be treated as an independent adult while the parents are still treating him at a child. At some point, too, parents start to wonder if their children are ever going to grow up and leave home. Some parents I talk to are ready for the empty nest and wonder how they can encourage their now twenty-something kids to leave.

QUESTION

My twenty-four-year-old has just returned home after living on his own for three years. He was just laid off from his job and needs our help. How should I handle this?

ANSWER

He's family; of course you want to help him, and having him live at home for a bit while he re-groups may be just the ticket. However, if he stays too long you may find yourself resenting his presence because you were used to having an empty nest and, after all, he's an adult.

The best way to offset this is to sit down with him and lay out your expectations about things like paying rent, helping with the chores, when and how often he can entertain. He should also let you know when he'll be away overnight or miss a meal. The second step is to work with him on a long-term plan. How long does he expect to live at home? What will he be doing to better his situation? Once you see him as a responsible adult living with you temporarily, you can likely enjoy this time with him.

QUESTION

My twenty-year-old is moving to another city and, while I know she's ready for the move, I want to do everything I can to help her in this transition.

ANSWER

Parents have mixed emotions when their children are ready to fly the nest. You're proud of her as she heads off to make her place in the world, but at the same time you're worried about her and will miss her dreadfully. From the day she was born, you've been moving toward this day. She needs to know that you trust her, that you're pleased for her and that you'll miss her. Give her permission to have fun, try new ideas and grow in her own way. She needs to know that you don't expect her to live exactly like you but that you do expect she'll become her own person, making choices about her lifestyle. Stay in touch. Some parents and children find that a regular time for phone calls works well; others use email and still others, snail mail. And, of course, let her know that if she needs advice or a friendly ear, you're there for her. It's okay to send care packages from time to time.

CHAPTER 11

GOOD JUDGMENT TAKES PRACTICE

Recently, I came across this handout from the Canadian Association of Family Resource Programs. It really spoke to me. It was as if the author had read the book you're now reading and understood it. So, with their permission, I want to share it with you.

Of course, it helps that I'm also a strong supporter of Family Resource Programs. Whether you call them Parent and Tot, Family Drop-In or Family Resource Program, they're the neighborhood gathering place for many parents and caregivers at home with babies and toddlers.

GOOD JUDGMENT TAKES PRACTICE

In a world where teens and young adults face many choices, parents want children to develop their thinking skills so that they learn to make good decisions. You can use everyday opportunities to teach decision-making and, most important, to give children chances to practice.

CHILD-LED PLAY

Playtime is perfect for letting children practice decision-making in areas where the choice matters little to adults. Children can choose for themselves which color block goes on the top of the tower, what gets served at the dolls' tea party or whether they play on the swings or the slide at the park.

OFFER CHOICES

Even very young children can start making simple choices: which glass they'll drink their juice from, which shoe to put on first. Choices get more elaborate as the child gets older: what clothes to wear to school, at what time to do homework.

SET LIMITS

Parents need to determine the limits within which choices get made. For instance, your child can choose to go to bed in red pajamas or blue pajamas, but you set the bedtime. Your child may choose what gift to buy for a friend's birthday, but you decide on the price range. Your children's ages and their individual abilities will influence which decisions you allow them to make.

ASK QUESTIONS

Parents can ask questions to stimulate children to think about the factors that go into making a choice. For example, if your child is deciding what to wear today, you could ask questions about the weather and the planned activities. Is it raining? What is the temperature? Do you think it will be warmer later in the day? Will you be playing outside? Your own experience will tell you what things you need to ask questions about. If you dictate the choices, the child won't learn or practice the steps in the process.

TEACH INFORMATION GATHERING

Sometimes a child doesn't yet know how to get the information that's required. In the above example of dressing for the weather, you could show your child how to read the thermometer or find the weather forecast on TV or radio or in the newspaper. There will also be times when you'll be the one to supply the information, and they can decide how to use it.

PRACTICE WITH STORIES

You can encourage thinking about the consequences of choices when you read books or tell stories to your children. Ask them what they think will happen next, what would have happened if the character had done something different, what they would do in that situation.

GIVE RESPONSIBILITY

When you let children decide for themselves, they may make choices different from yours. This is why it's important to set limits and give them responsibility for decisions in cases when you can live with their choices, even if you don't agree. If you can't stand the thought that they might eat dessert without finishing their main course, make everything in their lunch box equally nutritious.

ALLOW CONSEQUENCES

Giving responsibility also means allowing children to experience the consequences of their actions. Sometimes these consequences will be uncomfortable for children, and it may be hard as a parent to see your children unhappy. However, if you rescue them, you send them the message that it doesn't matter what decision they make, their parents will fix anything that goes wrong.

RESIST FEELING INCOMPETENT

Sometimes, when you let your children make their own choices, other people will blame you for what goes wrong. You'll be held responsible for decisions that your children make, whether you agree with their choices or not. That's why parents whose preschoolers choose to match a striped shirt with polka dot pants wear a button that says, "My child dressed himself today!" It takes strength and conviction to stand up to this attitude from others. A sense of humor helps too. Perhaps there should be a button for parents of teens: "My child paid for getting her hair dyed purple with her own money."

BE PATIENT

Learning to make good decisions takes time, and mistakes along the way are part of the learning process. As Mark Twain observed, "Good judgment comes from experience. And where does experience come from? Experience comes from bad judgment." It takes patience to raise a thinking child.

By Betsy Mann

NOTES FROM KATHY'S CHILDREN

We're Kathy's children, Chelsea and Foley. Mom has asked us to tell you a bit about our experiences moving out, I guess because she thinks we'll end up admitting she and Dad did a good job raising us!

Chelsea: In Mom's first book, *Who's in Charge Anyway?*, there's a part in which she talks about sitting down with Dad when she was pregnant with me and discussing what they wanted for their children. One of the things they mentioned is that they wanted their children to be capable. When I think back, they started that process immediately and in such small increments that my brother Foley and I never noticed.

Foley: The first example of this that I remember is preparing to go to kindergarten. We lived close to the school, and there were no busy roads so I could walk to school. We practiced on the weekend before school started, and then I walked to school by myself starting on the first day. Now, I'm sure that Mom followed me a bit the first few times to make sure I was okay, but I never knew about it. All I knew was that I was able to get myself to and from school and it was my responsibility to do so. That was the case all through elementary school.

Chelsea: In grade seven, I went to a new school about seven kilometers away. It was too far to walk so I took a school bus which stopped at the end of the street. Now, it was my responsibility to get up, get dressed, have breakfast, make my lunch and get to the bus stop on time. The bus came really early, and nobody else had to get up that early to get to work or school so I got myself up. Some of my friends were absolutely outraged that my mom didn't get up early to make sure that I was up on time, but why should she? At twelve years old is it too much to ask that a kid be able to set their alarm and get up for school on time? Of course, I did miss the bus once early in the year, and ended up riding my bike to school. That simple lesson taught me both consequences and responsibility. And for the rest of the year, I managed to get up on time.

Foley: The layering of responsibilities occurred in many ways. For example, when I was fifteen and Chelsea was sixteen, and she had her driver's license, Mom and Dad went away for a long weekend and left us alone. Now, they had been leading up to this gradually with overnight trips away and a friend of the family who was available in case we needed anything. This first "long" trip was a bit of an eye-opener. Since Chelsea had gotten her driver's license, she had done some of the family grocery shopping by herself, with a list and a check from Mom. This time, they left Chelsea and me with some money so we could order pizza one night, and a check so we could go grocery shopping to feed ourselves for the other few days. Very smart. Not only did we learn a bit about meal planning and grocery shopping, they also saved themselves from hearing us complain about there being "no food" in the fridge (a common complaint of teenagers).

Chelsea: On one of these first trips, our cat got into some oil-based paint the neighbor left out, and we had to call the vet and take the cat to the clinic in the middle of the night. But we did it. If we had an adult staying with us to take care of us, the adult would have handled the whole thing and we wouldn't have learned that we can take care of things by ourselves.

Foley: When you get right down to it, my mother is a softie. But she does practice what she preaches, so when it came time to send me off to university, she did so knowing, intellectually, that I could take care of myself, but, emotionally, she must have felt like a cruel mother. For those of us who attended university in a new town, there were many whose parents came along for the trip to help with finding and furnishing accommodation, getting set up and registered at school, and dealing with all those little things that you have to deal with for the first time. Not my Mom—she knew I could handle it myself even if I didn't know that I could.

Chelsea: I remember spending most of the summer after high school planning things such as finding a place to live (a classmate of mine was also going to Montreal so we decided to be room-mates) and deciding what to bring with me. It was only in August sometime when I sat back and thought, "Oh my good-ness, I'm moving OUT!" In hindsight I suppose that shows I had most of the tools I needed to take care of myself because some of my friends who were also moving away for school spent most of the summer worrying about how to get themselves to classes on time, how to make sure they scheduled their workload properly, and for those who weren't going to be living in residence, how they were going to feed themselves. Those day-to-day things never occurred to me because I already knew I could do that part.

Foley: I wasn't accepted for student residence, so I had to find an apartment. Luckily, I was able to stay with an uncle just out-side of town until I got settled. It was amazing—a completely new city, and suddenly responsibilities I'd never had before. The first thing I realized is that my sense of direction wasn't as good as I thought. Being from Vancouver, I learned at an early age that you could always find north by just looking for the mountains. I quickly realized that this doesn't translate to other cities. The next thing I realized is that people sometimes lie when it comes to renting out rooms. I finally settled on a room in a "large man-sion-like house." I don't know about mansion-like, but the cinder block and two-by-four shelving had a certain aesthetic appeal.

Chelsea: Now, don't get me wrong, I didn't just move on into the world without a care, and have everything work out great. That would be unrealistic. I did have some trial-and-error moments with budgeting monthly expenses—mostly involving running out of money before running out of the month. Because I didn't just have a blank check from Mom to do my grocery shopping, I did have to learn about buying things on sale and buying produce in season (a lesson learned when I almost bought a three dollar tomato in Montreal in the middle of winter).

Foley: Things worked out in the end. There were missteps, but I found a place to live. I found my way to school, and I figured out how to manage my time. My first experience moving out and going to university was great, and in the end I think I learned almost as much about myself and what I was capable of as I did in class.

Chelsea: Thinking about moving out, and how prepared I was (and wasn't), is actually a very interesting exercise because at the time, I didn't really think about the fact that I was moving "out" as much as that I'd be going to university, living in a different city, learning my way around a new place and making new friends. So I didn't move out without a care or concern, but I did have enough skills to get myself places, feed, clothe and house myself and figure out the rest. Oh yeah, and I also called home for advice on a regular basis. In fact, I still do!

INDEX

ABOUT THE AUTHOR

KATHY LYNN, BC, CCFE

The Leading parenting education speaker in Canada, Kathy Lynn is a professional speaker, broadcaster and author. She is a Certified Canadian Family Educator as well as the Parenting Education Advisor to the Council of Parent Participation Preschools of BC.

Her company, Parenting Today Productions Inc., has offered thousands of quality parenting education seminars, workshops, and keynote addresses to parents and professionals.

She is the author of *Who's in Charge, Anyway? How Parents Can Teach Children to Do the Right Thing* and a regular columnist with *Today's Parent* magazine and the *North Shore News*.

She has recorded three of her most popular workshops: Discipline ... Steps to Success, "Stop It, You Two" and I Like Me.